Australian & New Zealand Edition

Successful Job Interviews

FOR

DUMMIES®

A Wiley Brand

by Joyce Lain Kennedy

Successful Job Interviews For Dummies®

Australian and New Zealand Edition published by
Wiley Publishing Australia Pty Ltd
42 McDougall Street
Milton, Qld 4064
www.dummies.com

Copyright © 2014 Wiley Publishing Australia Pty Ltd

Original English language edition text and art *Job Interviews For Dummies*,
4th Edition, Copyright © 2012 by John Wiley & Sons, Inc., Hoboken, New Jersey.

The moral rights of the author have been asserted.

National Library of Australia
Cataloguing-in-Publication data:

Author:	Kennedy, Joyce Lain.
Title:	Successful Job Interviews For Dummies / Joyce Lain Kennedy.
Edition:	Australian and New Zealand ed.
ISBN:	9780730308058 (pbk.)
	9780730308089 (ebook)
Series:	For Dummies
Notes:	Includes index.
Subjects:	Employment interviewing — Australia.
	Employment interviewing — New Zealand.
Dewey Number:	650.144

Cover image: © Jamie Grill Photography/Getty Images

Typeset by diacriTech, Chennai, India

Printed in Singapore by
C.O.S. Printers Pte Ltd

10 9 8 7 6 5 4 3 2 1

Contents at a Glance

Table of Contents

Introduction

*I*f you'd rather fight off an alien invasion than be grilled in an interview, take heart — you've come to the right book. With the help of dozens of interviewing authorities, I make your interviewing challenge easy, successful, and even fun.

I share with you lots of new things in this Australian and New Zealand edition of *Successful Job Interviews For Dummies*, ranging from the cosmic shift sparked by the rise of social media that changes what networking means, to increasingly popular video interviewing that changes how communication occurs.

What hasn't changed is the fundamental role in the employment process played by job interviews — those crucial meetings that seal the deal on who gets hired and who gets left on the outside looking in.

Remember that job interviews are a slice of performance art. They're staged theatrical sketches rather than in-depth investigations into life histories. That's why theatre and drama are comparisons used throughout this book, and I hope you have some enjoyable moments with the show-biz motif.

With the help of this book, you, too, can put in a Show Stopper performance — one that wins so much enthusiastic, prolonged applause that the show is temporarily interrupted until the audience quiets down.

Successful Job Interviews For Dummies, Australian and New Zealand edition, is packed with the essentials of performing Show Stopper interviews:

- ✔ Strategies and techniques
- ✔ Sample dialogue and research tips
- ✔ The best answers to make-or-break questions

About This Book

A book of contemporary interview arts, *Successful Job Interviews For Dummies* contains the distilled wisdom of hundreds of leading interview experts whose brains I've been privileged to pick for many years. By absorbing the guidance and tips I pass on in this book, you can interview your way into a job by outpreparing and outperforming the other candidates.

To assist your navigation, I've established the following conventions:

- ✓ I use *italic* for emphasis and to highlight either new words or terms I define.

- ✓ Web addresses appear in a special font to distinguish them from the regular type in the paragraph.

- ✓ Sidebars, which are shaded boxes of text, consist of information that's interesting but not necessarily critical to your understanding of the topic.

I use the following terminology to label specific roles and organisations:

- ✓ A *candidate* or *job seeker* is a person applying for a job. (*Applicant* means the same thing.)

- ✓ An *interviewer* is someone interviewing a candidate for a job. An *interviewee* is a candidate being interviewed for a job.

- ✓ A *human resources* (or *HR*) *specialist*, *HR manager* or *screener* is an employer sentry who is conducting a screening (preliminary) interview.

- ✓ A *hiring manager*, *hiring authority*, *decision-maker*, *decision-making manager* or *department manager* is a management representative conducting a selection interview who has the authority to actually hire a person for a specific position.

- ✓ A *company*, *employer* or *organisation* is the entity you hope to work for, whether private and profit-making, or private and non-profit, or within the public sector.

- ✓ A *recruiter* (also called a *headhunter*) is an intermediary between the employer and you. *Internal recruiters* work inside the company, either as regular employees of the human resources department or as contract employees. *Third-party recruiters* or *independent recruiters* are external recruiters, some of whom are engaged on an ongoing basis so know the employer organisation very well while others are engaged just for a one-off hiring recruitment campaign and are paid only when a candidate they submit is hired.

✔ A *career coach* (also called a *career consultant)* helps job seekers gain workplace opportunities. (A *career counsellor* and a career coach represent two different professions, although their work sometimes overlaps.)

✔ A *hiring professional* is any of the aforementioned professionals who is engaged internally or externally in the employment process.

Foolish Assumptions

I assume you picked up this book for one or more of the following reasons:

✔ You've never been through a competitive interview and you're freaking out. You need a couple thousand friendly pointers from someone who's interviewed many of the marquee minds in the job interview business and lived to write about it.

✔ You've been through a competitive interview and assume the company sank like Atlantis because you never heard a peep from those folks again. Or maybe you could have done better and actually heard back if you'd have known more about what you were doing in this interview thing.

✔ The most important interview of your career is coming up. You realise that now is the hour to dramatically improve your interviewing success. You need help, and you're willing to learn and work for success.

✔ You've been through a slew of job interviews over the course of your career and have a hunch that some important things have changed (you just don't know what exactly). You want to catch up with the help of a trusted resource.

I further assume that you're someone who likes reliable, comprehensive information that gets to the point without rocking you to sleep. And I assume even further that you like your expertise with a smile now and then.

Icons Used in This Book

For Dummies signature icons are the little pictures you see in the margins of the book. I use them to focus on key bits of information. Here's a list of the icons you find in this book:

A bad review for a poor performance. This icon signals situations in which you may find trouble if you don't make a good decision.

This icon flags news you can use that you won't want to forget.

Bravo! This icon heralds star-quality lines and moves that prompt job offers.

Advice and information that can put you on award-winning pathways in your interview follow this icon. It lets you in on interviewing best practices.

Stop! Watch out! Read these warnings carefully.

Beyond the Book

In addition to the material in the print or ebook you're reading right now, *Successful Job Interviews For Dummies*, Australian and New Zealand edition, also comes with some access-anywhere resources on the internet. Check out the free Cheat Sheet at www.dummies.com/cheatsheet/successfuljobinterviewsau for some quick, helpful tips. For free extra companion material for this book, visit www.dummies.com/extras/successfuljobinterviewsau.

Where to Go from Here

On the stress scale of life, job interviewing ranks with making a speech before 500 people when you can't remember your name or why you're standing in a spotlight at a podium. The spot where you start in this book depends on your present needs:

✔ If you have a job interview tomorrow, quickly read Chapter 1 for an overview, followed by Chapters 20 and 21 for an instant infusion of key know-how. Additionally, go to the company's website to glean as much basic information as you can. Don't forget to read the company's press releases.

✔ When you have a few days before you're scheduled for an interview, read Chapter 1 and then flip through the Table of Contents to the chapters dealing with your most pressing concerns. Pay attention to Chapter 11, which reveals how to stack the deck in your favour during the closing minutes of your interview.

✔ When you have plenty of time, read the book from cover to cover. Practice recommended strategies and techniques. After you master the information in these pages, you'll have a special kind of insurance policy that pays big dividends for as long as you want to work.

Part I
Getting Started with Job Interviews

getting started
with

job
interviews

In this part...

✔ Understand why interviews are similar to acting and what this means to you as the interviewee.

✔ Become adept at screening interviews, whether by phone, in person or using automated systems, and breeze through to the next stage.

✔ Get ready for your in-person interview and get a handle on video interviewing, whether it's used for a screening or selection interview.

✔ Master interviews no matter what type you encounter — focusing on the objective, the type of interviewer or the technique used.

Chapter 1

Honing Your Job Interview Skills

In This Chapter

▶ Seeing how job interviewing is like acting

▶ Spotting what's new in interviewing

▶ Applying seven concepts to make you stand out

▶ Putting into practice ideas that make a good impression

A resume or profile functions as bait to snag a job interview. The interview is the decisive event when a hiring authority decides whether you'll be offered the job.

Because the job interview is such an important part of getting a job — and you may not have interviewed in awhile — any number of unfortunate scenarios may be sneaking into your unconscious, including fears of these confidence-disturbers:

> ✔ Stumbling and mumbling your way through the ordeal
>
> ✔ Being glued to a hot seat as they sweat the answers out of you
>
> ✔ Forgetting your interviewer's name (or the last place you worked)

Exhale. You've come to the right book. Take the suggestions within these pages to heart and you'll head into every interview feeling confident, calm and well prepared. What more can you ask?

Note: This first chapter serves as an overview for the entire book. The pages that follow are wide and deep, with details that can help you gain a lifetime of confidence in your ability to sail through the drama of interviews and secure the best job offers.

Being the Successful Candidate

When you're engaged in a selection interview, your entire future may rest on how successful you are in presenting yourself to a stranger across a desk in 15, 30 or 60 minutes. Making life-altering decisions during this micro slice of time isn't real life — it's a performance.

The most successful interviews for you require solid preparation to rehearse what you want to say, showing your future bosses that you're smart and quick on the uptake, as well as able to communicate and not likely to jump the tracks.

At each meeting, your goal is to deliver a flawless performance that rolls off your tongue and gets the employer applauding — and remembering — you. Perfect candidate, you!

But what about all the people who tell you, 'Just be yourself and you'll do fine in your interview'? That advice doesn't always work for you when it comes to job interviewing.

Why 'be yourself' can be poor advice

The bromide 'be yourself' is very difficult to articulate with consistency. Be yourself? Which self? Who is the real you? Our roles change at various times.

Your role: Job seeker

Jerry is a father, an engineer, a marathon runner, a public speaker, a law student at night and a writer of professional papers. Jennifer is a loving daughter, the best salesperson in her company, a pilot, a tennis player, a rugby fan and a history buff.

But at this time in their lives, Jerry and Jennifer — like you — are job seekers. Similarly, the stranger across an interviewing desk is in the role of interviewer.

Getting real about the job seeker role

Playing the role most appropriate to you at a given time, and playing it effectively enough to get you the job you deserve, isn't turning your back on authenticity. To do less than play the role of a hard-charging job seeker courts unemployment — or underemployment.

Why 'be natural' can be poor advice

First-cousin advice urging you to 'be yourself' in a job interview is the 'be natural' admonition. On the whole, isn't natural better than artificial? Not always.

Is combed hair natural? Shaved legs? Trimmed beard? Polished shoes? How about covering a cough in public? Or not scratching where you itch?

Being natural in a job interview is fine as long as you don't use your desire to be natural and authentic as an excuse to display your warts or blurt out negative characteristics.

Never treat a job interview as a confessional in which you're obligated to disclose imperfections, indiscretions or personal beliefs that don't relate to your future job performance.

In job interviews, every minute counts in the getting-to-know-you game. And to really know someone in a brief encounter of 15, 30 or 60 minutes is simply impossible. Instead of real life, each participant in an interview sees what the other participant(s) wants seen. If you doubt that, think back: How long did you need to really get to know your flatmate, spouse or significant other?

If you insist on being natural, an employer may pass you over because of your unkempt beard or unshined shoes, or because you don't feel like smiling that day.

What exactly is a Show Stopper in job interviewing?

In the drama of job interviewing, a Show Stopper performance causes the interviewer to mentally shout, 'Bravo! More!' Your stunning impact quickly translates to a preliminary decision in your favour. If follow-up interviews, testing and reference checking support that reaction, a job offer is on its way to you. The employer may continue to see other candidates to round out the interview process but, in reality, no-one else stands a chance of landing the job after you figuratively stop the show.

The things you've done to date — your identification of
your skills, your resume and profile, your cover letter, your
networking, your social media efforts — are all wasted if you fail
to deliver a job interview that produces a job offer.

Make the most of your critical brief encounters by learning
the skills of storytelling, using body language, establishing rapport
and doing more of what's in this modern interview book.

New Faces, New Factors in Interviewing

Are you having trouble staking out your future because you can't
close the sale during job interviews? This mangled proverb states
the right idea: *If at first you don't succeed . . . get new batteries.*

Recharge yourself with knowledge of the new technology and
trends that are affecting job interviews. Here are highlights of
the contemporary job interview space.

Interviewing in the digital age

Classic interviewing skills continue to be essential to job search
success, but more technological firepower is needed in a world
growing increasingly complex, interconnected and competitive.

The new tech trends revolutionise all components of the job
search, including the all-important job interview. Here are
examples of technological newcomers and how they change
interviewing practices:

- ✔ **Video interviews:** Both live and recorded video job
  interviews are coming of age, requiring that you acquire
  additional skills and techniques to make the cut. Chapter 3
  is a primer on how you can outflank your competition by
  presenting like a pro in video interviews.

- ✔ **Phone interviews:** Automated and recorded phone
  screening services permit employers to ask up to a dozen
  canned screening questions and allow candidates up to two
  minutes to answer each question. Informed interviewees
  anticipate the questions and must hit their marks the first
  time because you don't get the chance to go again with
  recorded answers. Read about this technology in Chapter 2.

✔ **Credibility:** Credibility issues are surfacing for multitalented job seekers (or those with a chequered work background) who, by posting various resumes and profiles online, come across as different people with different skill sets. This development can be a knockout punch for you in a tight job market where employers have plenty of candidates on offer. Sidestep the emerging problem of identity contradictions in interviews by following the advice offered in Chapter 14.

✔ **Web woes:** Employers can hire experts to scour the internet and social media (such as LinkedIn, Facebook and Twitter) to check out your online history. Such a service rakes through closed databases in the deep web, leaving virtually no secrets unrevealed. If the deep web reveals negative information, you may get a chance to defend yourself in an interview — or you may never know why you struck out. See Chapter 14 for more information on this digital sleuthing tool.

Expect new kinds of interviewers

If the last time you trod the boards of job interviewing you went one to one with a single interviewer, usually a white man or woman, get ready for a different set of questioners, like these possibilities:

✔ A veteran team of six managers — individually or collectively

✔ A hiring manager (especially in technical and retail fields) who is two decades younger than you

✔ Someone of a different background or heritage

Turn to Chapter 4 for a broader picture of group interviews, and to Chapter 13 for a good tip on interviews with younger bosses.

Showcase your ability to hit the ground running. Because the new norm is staying in a job only for a few years — or, in contract assignments, a few months — the hiring spotlight lasers in on the competencies and skills you can use from Day One. The question is, *What can you do for our company immediately?*

You can come across as ready to blast off if you do enough research on the company's goals (increase revenues, reduce costs, acquire new market share, land larger accounts, create a technical breakthrough), think about how you can help the company reach those goals, and remain ready to speak the insider jargon of the industry.

If the job you're applying for isn't at the professional or managerial level, research the nature of the company's business, assume that it wants to make or save money, and stock up on a few good buzzwords used in the industry.

Scope out more ways to show your launch speed in Chapter 5.

Overcome the job-hopping objection

The current employer-driven job market makes it easy for companies to buy into the 'job-hopper objection' and, as a matter of policy, turn away unemployed candidates and people who've held three jobs in five years. Unfortunately, many of these automatic rejects have been trapped in a cycle of frequent redundancy rounds, part-time work, temp assignments, seasonal employment, contract jobs, freelance gigs and company shutdowns.

Some companies refuse to hire so-called job hoppers, claiming that they'll quit before employers can get a return on their training investment — or that, if the unemployed candidates were any good, they'd be on someone's payroll.

What's a sincere, hard-working person to do? Try this quartet of basic rebuttals:

- ✔ **Say varied experience beats repeated experience.** Explain how your dynamic work history makes you a far more vibrant and resourceful contributor than if you'd been stationary for four years.

- ✔ **Briefly explain departures.** Give a reasonable, short, even-toned account of why you left each job. (Convey that it wasn't your fault without ever using that phrase.)

- ✔ **Review your accomplishments.** You can't change the amount of time you were on certain jobs, but you can divert the focus to your accomplishments and contributions. Employers are impressed by candidates who are good at what they do, even if they were only in a role for a short period of time.

✔ **Confirm interest in stable employment.** Forget the 'loyalty' chatter, but make a point of your intense interest in a stable opportunity where you can apply all your considerable know-how for the employer's benefit.

Chapter 17 offers more suggestions on how to maximise the value of your experience.

Learn new lines for small-business jobs

Have you grown up professionally in a large-company environment? If so, carefully consider the answers you give when applying to small companies. Such a move can happen sooner than you think if you're forced into an involuntary change of employment. Prime-timers in droves are discovering that the small business sector is where the action is for them.

Emphasise different aspects of your work personality than the ones you emphasise when interviewing for a big company. Interviewers at big companies and small companies have different agendas.

Among the reasons owners of small ventures reject former big-company people are these stereotypical perceptions: People who come out of Big Corporate often are thought to be

✔ Unaware of the needs of small business

✔ Too extravagant in their expectations of resources and compensation

✔ Too spoiled to produce double the work product their former jobs required

✔ Unwilling to wear more than one job hat at a time

✔ Deadwood, or they wouldn't have been cut loose from the big company

Chapters 13, 15 and 16 can help you with this issue.

Polish your storytelling skills

Behaviour-based interviewing is said to predict future performance based on past performance in similar situations. The behavioural interviewing style isn't new, but it seems to be more popular than ever.

Advocates of the behavioural style claim that it is 55 per cent predictive of future on-the-job behaviour, compared to traditional interviewing, at only 10 per cent predictive. The reasoning is, 'If you acted a certain way once, you'll act that way again.' Solid proof of this claim is hard to come by. But for you as a job seeker, it doesn't matter the least bit whether the claim is true or false. The behavioural style is such a big deal with employers today that you need to know how to use the style to your advantage.

It works like this: Interviewers ask candidates to tell them a story of a time when they reacted to a certain situation. *How did you handle an angry customer? Describe an example of a significant achievement in your last job.* The more success stories you can drag in from your past, the more likely the interviewers using this approach will highly rate your chances of achieving equivalent success in the future.

Read more about behaviour-based interviewing in Chapter 4.

Focus on fitting in

'We chose another candidate who is a better job fit' is another familiar reason that seems to be heard today more often than before when explaining to a disappointed job seeker why someone else got the job.

In the workplace, 'fit' essentially refers to how an individual fits into a company's culture. Company culture is expressed in the values and behaviours of the group, which forms a kind of 'tribe' or, to use an analogy from high school, an 'in crowd'.

The culture typically flows from company or department chieftains: If the boss wears long sleeves, you wear long sleeves; if the boss shows a sense of humour, you show a sense of humour; if the boss works until after 6 pm, you work until after 6 pm.

When you're given the not-the-best-fit-for-the-job rejection, the reason is

- ✔ A convenient short and legally safe answer
- ✔ A cover story
- ✔ A belief that the hiring decision-makers perceive you won't fit in well with the 'tribe'

When the reason really is the fit issue, decision-makers may think that you can do the job but that you won't do it the way they want — and, furthermore, they just don't feel at ease with you.

Instead of losing sleep over a fit-based turndown, move on. Do better pre-interview research (see Chapter 5). At least you won't waste time on companies well known for being a fortress of round holes when you're a square peg.

Seven Concepts to Help You Win the Interview

You've heard it said over and over that you have only one chance to make a first impression. It's especially true for job interviewing, so make that first impression pay off. Read these seven super tips to make the hiring gods choose you at job interviews.

Go all out in planning ahead

Preparation makes all the difference in whether you get the best offers as you face intense scrutiny, field probing questions and reassure employers who are afraid of making hiring mistakes. You must show that you're tuned in to the company's needs, that you have the skills to get up to speed quickly and that you're a hand-in-glove fit with the company.

Fortunately, never in history has so much information about companies and industries been so easily accessible, both in print and online. Chapter 5 gives tonnes of tips on researching your audience.

Distinguish screening from selection interviews

As hiring action is increasingly concentrated in smaller companies, the separation between screening and selection interviews fades: The same person may do both types. But traditionally, here's how the types, which I cover in Chapter 4, differ.

Screening interviews

In large organisations, interviewing is usually a two-stage process. A screening specialist eliminates all candidates except the best qualified. The screening interview is usually conducted by telephone or video instead of face-to-face in the same room. Survivors are passed to a manager (or panel of managers) who selects the winning candidate.

Screeners are experienced interviewers who look for reasons to screen you out based on your qualifications. Screeners can reject, but they cannot hire. They won't pass you on to hiring managers if your experience and education don't meet the specifications of the job.

When you're being interviewed by a screener, be pleasant and neutral. Volunteer no strong opinions. Raise no topics, except to reinforce your qualifications. Answer no questions that aren't asked — don't look for trouble.

But do remember to smile a lot.

Selection interviews

By the time you're passed on to a hiring authority who makes the selection, you're assumed to be qualified or you wouldn't have made it that far along the channels of employment. You're in a pool of 'approved' candidates chosen for the selection interview.

At a selection interview, move from neutral into high gear if the person doing the interview will be your boss or colleague. No more bland behaviour — turn up the wattage on your personality power. This is the best time to find out whether you'll hit it off with the boss or colleagues, or fit into the company culture.

Verify early what they want and show how you deliver

Almost as soon as you're seated in a selection interview, ask the interviewer to describe the scope of the position and the qualifications of the ideal person for it.

Although you've already done this research when you're going for Show Stopper status, use this question to confirm your research. If you're wrong, you must know immediately that you need to shift direction.

(***Note:*** This super tip was shared with me by several career management experts.)

How can you adapt the tell-me-what-you-want tip when you're dealing with multiple interviewers? That's easy: Direct your question to the senior panel member and wait for an answer. Then gaze around the group and ask, 'Does anyone have something to add to the ideal person description?'

Confirming your research (or gaining this information on the spot) is the key to the entire interview. You now know for sure the factors upon which the hiring decision is made and how to target your answers.

Always ask questions of the interviewer (or interview panel) using a smile and conversational style so you don't sound like you are taking over and directing the interview process.

Connect all your qualifications with a job's requirements

If a quick glance at your notes reminds you that the interviewer missed a requirement or two listed in the job posting when describing the position's scope and the ideal person for it, help the interviewer by tactfully bringing up the missing criteria yourself. Keep it simple:

> *I see from my notes that your posting asked for three years of experience. I have that and two years more, each with a record of solid performance in ...*

You want to demonstrate that you take this job possibility seriously, an attitude that the employer will applaud. Winning job offers by targeting your interview performance to a company's requirements is a logical follow-up to the resume targeting strategy (see *Writing Resumes & Cover Letters For Dummies*, 2nd Australian and New Zealand Edition, John Wiley & Sons, for more).

Memorise short-form sales statements about yourself

Almost certainly, you will be asked to respond to some version of the 'tell me about yourself' question (see Chapter 14). You're not helping your hiring chances if you respond with a question that a 13-year-old might ask: 'What do you want to know?' That naïve approach makes you sound unprepared.

Instead, commit to memory a short-form sales statement (two minutes max, and preferably less than one minute) that describes your education, experience and skills, and matches your strengths to the jobs you seek.

Some people call such a statement a 'commercial', while others prefer the terms 'elevator speech' or 'career profile summary'. Whatever you call it, after briefly reciting the facts of your background, make your statement sizzle by adding a couple of personality sentences about such traits as your curiosity, commitment and drive to succeed.

The 'personal branding brief' is another version of the short-form sales statement. Used chiefly by professionals, managers and executives, it's incorporated into all self-marketing opportunities, including job interviewing.

In personal branding, you become known for something — *The Chaser* boys for political satire and Karrie Web for golfing, for example. You don't have to be famous to pursue personal branding, but you do have to be consistent in your efforts to develop your brand.

Your goal is to perfect a *branding brief* that tells your 'story' — one that rolls off your tongue — in about 20 to 30 seconds, or in 100 words or less:

> *After I graduated from Victoria University in Wellington, I worked in the insurance industry until I took a break to start a family. That accomplished, I went back for refresher education. Now, thoroughly updated, I'm looking for a new connection in either the insurance or financial fields.*

 The difference between a commercial and a branding brief is length and content. A commercial is longer and includes more details than a cut-to-the-chase branding brief.

Win two thumbs up from the hiring manager, and you're in!

Likeability is a huge factor in choosing and keeping employees, as I note later in this chapter. Given a choice of technically qualified applicants, employers almost always choose the one they like best. For your purposes, remember this: *We like people who are like us.*

How do you encourage the interviewer to think, 'You and me against the problem' rather than 'You against me'?

Beyond exchanging pleasantries, establishing mutual interests, connecting with eye contact and other well-known bonding techniques, watch for special opportunities:

✔ Suppose your interviewer looks harried, with ringing telephones and people rushing about interrupting your talk. Flash a sympathetic smile and commiserate: *It looks like you're having one of those days.* The subtext of your comment is, *I understand your frustrations. I've been in a similar place. You and I are alike.*

✔ Or suppose you're showing a work sample. Ask if you can come around to the interviewer's side of the desk to discuss your sample. You're looking at it 'together'.

Forget about age, colour, gender or ethnic background. Do whatever you reasonably can to make the hiring manager believe the two of you are cut from similar cloth.

To rewrite the famous 20th-century Broadway wit and playwright Damon Runyon: *The part goes not always to those we like, nor the hiring to our twins, but that's the way to bet.*

Negotiating with strength

The time when you have the most power in the recruitment process is *after* you have been offered the job and *before* you have accepted it. In an ideal world you would leave the salary and benefits discussion until then.

In the real world the salary question could come up at the beginning of the first interview. If so, try not to commit to specifics. If asked about what you're currently earning you could choose to be honest but explain you don't feel your current salary is relevant because the job on offer is different in scope and level of responsibility. You could also research the salary level for the role you're interviewing for using recruitment websites and speak only in term of your expected salary range. Or you could offer to discuss salary once you know the full scope of the role. You need to walk the line between not appearing difficult by sidestepping the question and not short-changing yourself by coming up with a figure you think will please the recruiter or employer.

Also, saying that money isn't your most important consideration can signal to an employer that you will settle for less than what the role is really worth, so be careful using this line.

Admittedly, stalling salary talk until a better time is much more difficult today than it was a decade ago. But you should be holding out for the market value of the new job, not settling for an inadequate figure of your present or previous employment.

Only when you know the scope of the position and its market value — and that the company wants to hire you — are the stars in alignment to bargain in your best interest.

Read Chapter 7 for in-depth guidance on salary negotiation.

Interview Coaching Tips

Rookie? Prime-timer? Clerk? Chief executive officer? No matter. You can do exceptionally well by following certain performance routines that succeed in any interview scene. Some of these suggestions are basic and familiar, but most people who haven't been on the interview tour for awhile can use the reminders.

Play the likeability card

When you're up against a rigid requirement that you absolutely can't meet and that you're pretty sure is going to mean curtains for you in the interview, try this last-ditch compensatory response:

> Let's say that you were to make me an offer and I accept. What can I do when I start to further compensate for my lack of [requirement] as I work hard to relieve your immediate workload?

Essentially, you're counting on your likeability. You're asking the employer to revert to the philosophy of hiring for attitude and training for skill. You're using the likeability qualification to plug your requirement gap.

As legendary recruiting guru Paul Hawkinson observes: 'Likeability is a factor that can turn the tide in your direction. Although skill level and applicable experience trump at the beginning of the interview process, I've seen dozens of less-than-qualified people hired because the employer *liked* them better than the perfect candidate with the personality of a doorknob.'

Everyone likes to work with agreeable, sunny people. People rarely hire someone they don't like.

Soak up moves that make interviewers see you as an agreeable and calm person in Chapter 9.

Style your body language

Interviewers observe everything about you — not only your dress and interview answers, but also your body language, facial expressions, posture, carriage and gestures. If you're a rookie, think dignity. If you're a prime-timer, think energy. In between? Watch TV interviews with actors, political candidates and other public figures for hints of what looks good and what doesn't.

Confirm that your body language is sending the 'Hire me!' message with the tips in Chapter 9. Chapter 8's up-to-date data on dress and appearance add even more nonverbal firepower to your candidacy.

Be positive

Steer clear of negative words (such as *hate*, *don't ever want*, *absolutely not* and *refuse*). And avoid such risky topics as the knock-down, drag-out fights you had with that bonehead you used to work for — never knock the old boss. Your prospective new boss may empathise with your old boss and decide to never be your boss at all.

Chapter 6 throws more light on avoiding a maze of negativity and looking as though you're a serial complainer who will never be satisfied.

Winning candidates are memorable

Comparing TV reality talent show winners to job interview candidates, US career coach Joe Turner (www.jobsearchguy.com) says it's the total package that counts. 'You don't have to be the best singer or dancer — just the most *remembered* decent performer. Same for the job interview. You don't always have to be the best candidate with the top skills. You do have to find a way to be the most remembered hireable candidate.'

Start your interview on the right foot

Here are four tips to help you make a good impression right off the bat:

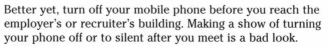

✔ Find out in advance what to wear (see Chapter 8) and where the interview site is located. Make a trial run, if necessary.

✔ Be on time or a few minutes early, be nice to the receptionist, read a business magazine while you're waiting and — surprise, surprise — don't smoke just before arriving, chew gum, make loud mobile phone calls or otherwise look as though you lack couth.

Better yet, turn off your mobile phone before you reach the employer's or recruiter's building. Making a show of turning your phone off or to silent after you meet is a bad look.

✔ Develop a couple of icebreaker sound bites, such as complimentary comments about the office, attractive colour scheme or interesting pictures.

✔ Don't sit until you're asked or until the interviewer sits. Don't offer to shake hands until the interviewer does.

During the interview, frequently use the interviewer's name (but never use a first name until you're invited to or the person has introduced themselves using only their first name). And remember to make a lot of eye contact by looking at the bridge of an interviewer's nose. (Divert your gaze occasionally, or you're perceived as more creepy than honest.)

Track down more suggestions for making yourself a memorable candidate in Chapter 10.

Remember that interviews are a two-way street

Communication skills are among the most desired qualities employers say they want. Answer questions clearly and completely. Be sure to observe all social skills of conversation — no interrupting, no profanity. Just as you shouldn't limit yourself to one- or two-word answers, neither should you try to cover your nervousness with surround-sound endless talking. Aim for a happy medium.

Surviving a snippy interviewer

Short of taking out a restraining order, what should you do when an interviewer's manner is offensive?

That depends on who's doing the talking. When the interviewer is the person who would be your boss, be certain that you're not misunderstanding intent. If conversation really is disrespectful, bail out unless you want to spend most of your waking hours dealing with a difficult person. Show class. Just say, 'Thank you for your time. I don't think this job is a good fit for me.' (*Payback:* It may leave the interviewer regretful that you're the good one who got away.)

But when the interviewer is doing preliminary screening, give the employer the benefit of the doubt by assuming that the interviewer doesn't represent the entire company and will be working five floors below you in a sub-basement. Here are a few coping techniques when responding to something offensive:

✔ Smile and make a light remark: 'Oh, do you think so? That bears watching.'

✔ Respond with a two-second non-answer, and then quickly ask a question: 'That's an interesting observation. It reminds me to ask you, what role would the person in this position play in the new company product launch?'

✔ Pretend the rude remark is a dropped call that you didn't hear, pause and talk about your accomplishments or skills.

✔ When an interviewer keeps interrupting or contradicting you, look puzzled and ask for clarification. 'Perhaps I'm not following you correctly. Can you please restate the question or explain what you mean by ___ ?'

When all else fails, remember the words of English writer JK Rowling, author of the *Harry Potter* books: 'Yet, sadly, accidental rudeness occurs alarmingly often. Best to say nothing at all, my dear man.'

Take in Chapter 14 for a savvy start on how to talk about yourself.

Agree to take pre-employment tests

No-one likes those annoying pre-employment tests. Job seekers keep hoping they'll drop off the face of the earth, but they're with us still. When you want the job, you're going to have to suck it up and test when asked. No test, no job.

Race to Chapter 6 for survival clues when you hope to be the last one standing after test time.

Fighting back on interview exploitation

You can lose your intellectual property through abuse of the job interview.

In the *performance interview* for professional and managerial jobs, candidates are required to prove themselves with projects that demonstrate on-the-job skills, problem-solving capabilities and communications abilities.

The employer asks for a proposal of how you would handle a company project or requests that you design a process the company can use. You're told to be ready to 'defend your ideas' at the interview.

Unfortunately, sometimes the free-sample demand is incredibly time-consuming (say, 80 hours) and costly ($200 and up in materials and research). You do your best, but suppose you don't get the job. In an example of shoddy ethics, your work samples may be given to the victorious candidate, who then steals your viable creative ideas. In the following sections, I give you a few examples from stung readers of my newspaper and web column.

Portfolio scam

When applying to an advertising agency for a copywriting job, the owner asked me to leave my portfolio for review. He kept the portfolio and called on all the clients whose work was shown in the portfolio! Since then, *I always respond to requests to leave or send my portfolio with this statement: 'I need to be there to clarify the work shown. I will be glad to bring it, and we can discuss my work at your convenience.'*

Consulting caper

My husband, an expert in human resources, spent two long days interviewing in a small town with the owner of a family company and his son. He gave them an unbelievable amount of advice and information to help their meagre HR program, process management and integrated product development. All we got out of that was reimbursement for a 200-mile car trip, a bad motel and meals. That was our first realisation of how small businesses, in particular, get almost-free consulting work.

Training trickery

I was a candidate for a city's new training division chief. I had to spend several hours in the city's computer labs designing programs and leaving them on CDs. I knew that, with my education and experience, I had done well.

A long-term firefighter with zero training experience got the job with the city and used my materials for new employees!

(continued)

(continued)

Protecting yourself

How do you avoid abuse without taking yourself out of the running for a job you want when you're not sure about the real interview agenda? Here are two ideas.

First, you can highlight the work is your copyright. Under Australia and New Zealand law, copyright lies in the work (that is, the expression of the ideas rather than the ideas themselves). Copyright resides with the author of the work and, importantly, is free and automatic upon creation of the work. So a copyright notice (©) isn't required to gain copyright, but is useful to highlight that you know the work is yours and can't be reproduced without your permission. Next to the copyright notice you can also add 'Confidential — Property of (Your Name)' on your plan's cover.

When you're desperate or really, really, really want the job but don't have the time, inclination or money to respond in full measure, offer something like this:

I'm glad that you see I have the brains and talent to bring value to your company. I'm happy, too, that you have the confidence in my work to ask me to handle such a potentially important solution to your marketing challenge. With my background, I'm sure I can do an outstanding job on this assignment. But you do realise, I hope, that such an important project would require 80 to 100 hours of intensely focused work. I'd enjoy doing it but, frankly, I have several other job interviews scheduled that I really can't shift around. Do you think a sample of substantially smaller scope would serve as well for your purposes?

With a statement like this, you

✔ Remind the interviewer that you're a top candidate

✔ Promise superior results

✔ Bring a reality check to a sensitive interviewer about what's being asked of you

✔ Let the interviewer know others are interested in you

✔ Propose to do much less work until a job offer crosses your palm

You can, of course, flatly refuse to part with advance goodies. In a seller's market, you'll probably be considered anyway. But in a buyer's market, the likelihood is that you'll be passed over when you decline to turn in a hefty free sample.

Keep your ears up and your eyes open

Don't just sell, sell, sell. Take time to listen. When you're constantly busy thinking of what you're going to say next, you miss vital points and openings. So work on your listening skills. When you don't understand an interviewer's question, ask for clarification.

Observe the interviewer's moves. Watch for three key signs: High interest (leaning forward), boredom (yawning or displaying a glazed look) or a devout wish to end the interview (stacking papers or standing up). After assessing where you stand with the interviewer, take the appropriate action:

- ✔ High interest suggests you're stopping the show and should continue.

- ✔ The remedy for boredom is to stop and ask, *Would you rather hear more about (whatever you've been talking about) or my skills in the ABC area?*

- ✔ When the interviewer is ready to end the meeting, first ask whether the interviewer has any reservations about your fit for the job; if so, attempt to erase them.

- ✔ Then go into your interview closing mode (see Chapter 11). Gain a sense of timing and keep the door open for follow-up contact by asking three questions: *What is the next step in the hiring process? When do you expect to make a decision? May I feel free to call if I have further questions?*

Chapter 2

Getting Past Screening Interviews

. . . .

In This Chapter

▶ Understanding screening as the first step towards selection

▶ Cutting to the chase and engaging with a screener

▶ Getting through automated screening systems

▶ Surviving computer screening

. . . .

*N*ot understanding how screening practices work in today's recruiting industry is keeping many good people on the sidelines when jobs are handed out.

Under the watchful eye of James M Lemke, headliner in the human resource trenches and one of this book's technical advisors, this chapter gives you the fundamentals of modern screening practices to help you survive being 'screened out'. (Additionally, see Chapter 4 for the big picture on different types of interviews and how they relate to each other.)

Two Basic Steps in Job Interviewing

Most employers that are large enough to have a human resources department split the hiring function into two steps: Screening and selection. These work as follows:

▶ *Screening interviews* are Step 1 in choosing someone for a job. Designed to narrow the candidate pool for the managers who make the hiring decisions, screening interviews weed out unqualified candidates. If you don't get past Step 1, you're out of the running.

A screening interview is typically conducted by an employee in the employer's human resources department (often a support person or a junior recruiter) or by an outside recruiting firm engaged by the employer.

Your goal in a screening interview is to show that your qualifications fit the employer's bill. You're not quizzing the interviewer about job suitability for factors important to you, but keeping yourself in the running for the job.

✔ *Selection interviews* are Step 2 in choosing someone for a job. Selection interviews provide a wider and deeper evaluation of qualified candidates who survive screening interviews. (Selection interviews are also called *hiring interviews*.)

A selection interview is typically conducted by one or more managers to whom the new hire will report. Sometimes it includes potential colleagues as well.

Asking questions about the company is appropriate in a selection interview. (Find questions to ask about the company in Chapter 10.)

Hot News about Screening Interviews

In a frigid job market, job seekers experience a heat wave of screening interviews.

The uptick in a rush to discard unqualified candidates makes sense. The trend can be explained by digital traffic jams caused by the mobs of people who 'spray and pray'. The spray-and-pray theory is that if you apply for every open job within reach, qualified or not, you're sure to land one. (This hope is misplaced, akin to counting on the lottery as a retirement plan.)

The tight job market means employers and recruiters are usually inundated with a tonne of applications from both unqualified as well as suitable candidates. In response, employers have developed an understandable preference to cut to the chase as a strategy to save both time and money. The initial focus of a recruitment campaign is usually on screening applicants *out* rather than *in* and so for this reason your first contact with a company will most likely be with a screener.

Confusing term

To keep terms confusing, if not amusing, screening interviews are sometimes called *screeners*. The people who conduct them are also sometimes called *screeners*. Hey, I didn't make this up!

Screeners can't hire you. But they can keep you from being hired. Give a screener enough information about your qualifications to satisfy the job's requirements. Engage! Go all in to help the screener connect the dots from the job to you.

Screening interviews come in three basic models:

- ✔ Human screening (usually conducted by telephone)
- ✔ Automated phone screening options
- ✔ Online screening questionnaire

Sounding Qualified on the Phone

Even though talking on the phone gives a casual impression, you need to present yourself as a qualified professional for the job you want.

Because most people don't prepare for screening phone interviews as rigorously as they prepare for face-to-face meetings, the casualty fallout is heavy. The telephone 'screen call' can come at any time, day or night.

If surprises aren't your thing, stick to the steps I outline in the upcoming sections.

Mobile phones and smartphones have become the norm in a mobile world, but they still suffer from too many 'Can you hear me now?' moments to be your first choice for a life-altering event like a screening interview. Generally, landline phones of good quality remain the most reliable for excellent audio quality.

Phone interview essentials

Stash one phone in a quiet room stocked with all your interview essentials. Must-haves include:

- ✔ Your current resume (preferably customised to the job you're discussing)
- ✔ A list of your professional accomplishments
- ✔ Background information on the employer
- ✔ Questions about the company and position
- ✔ Outlines of brief stories that illustrate your qualifications and problem-solving abilities
- ✔ A calendar, with all scheduled commitments and open dates
- ✔ A notepad, pen and calculator
- ✔ Water and tissues

Make phone appointments

Screeners sometimes purposely try to catch you with your guard down, hoping surprise strips away the outer layers of your preparation and that you'll blurt out genuine, unrehearsed thoughts and feelings. They may see unanticipated calls as useful for measuring your ability to think on your feet.

But you want to avoid giving answers from a brain frozen on standby status, right? Whenever possible, don't answer stuff on the fly when a call comes in. You won't be prepared and you won't do your best. Schedule an appointment for your phone interview. Say that you're walking out the door to a meeting across town and will call back as quickly as you can.

> *Thank you for calling. I appreciate your attention. I'm very interested in speaking with you about my qualifications. Unfortunately, this is not a good time for me — I'm headed out the door. Can I call you back in an hour or two? Or would tomorrow be better?*

Phone interviewing when you're at work

When your current employer doesn't know that you're looking for a new job, close the door and speak to the interviewer for only a couple of minutes. Ask the caller if you can set up an in-person interview right then — or if you can talk in the evening when you're at home.

If a recruiter insists on calling you back rather than the other way around, do what you would do for any other interview: Be ready early as a reminder to interview as a professional. Change out of your jeans and into the type of dress you'd wear in a business meeting. Most importantly, treat the call as an overture to an in-room meeting that you're going to snag by doing an excellent job on your screener.

Project your winning image

When the call comes, heed the following suggestions, most of which come from Mark S James, a leading executive career coach (www.hireconsultant.com):

- ✔ **If you have a home office, use it because it's businesslike.** You may find it helpful to face a blank wall to eliminate distractions of gazing out a window or spotting dust on your favourite painting.

- ✔ **Gather essential information.** At the start of the conversation, get the caller's name, title, company, email address and phone number. Read back the spelling.

- ✔ **Market yourself.** Assume the role of 'seller' during the interview. If you sell your skills and abilities effectively, the listener sees value in bringing you in for an interview.

- ✔ **Strike the right tone.** Be enthusiastic, but don't dominate the conversation.

- ✔ **Have an answer ready.** Be prepared to answer the 'tell me about yourself' request early on; keep your answer to two minutes. (You find strategic techniques for handling this key question in Chapter 14.)

- ✔ **Don't rush or drone on.** Speak clearly and be aware of your pace — not too fast, not too slow. Don't ramble. Keep your answers short and succinct; if the interviewer wants more information, she'll ask for it.

- ✔ **Use check-back phrases.** After answering a question, you can add such follow-on phrases as, *Does that answer your question? Have I sufficiently answered your question about my managerial experience? Is this the kind of information you're seeking?*

- ✔ **Be a champion listener.** Prove that you're paying attention by feeding back what the interviewer says: *In other words, you feel that* ... Interject short responses intermittently to acknowledge the interviewer's comments: *That's interesting ... I see ... great idea.*

- ✔ **Get specific.** Describe your ability to benefit the company by using specific dollar amounts and percentages to explain your past accomplishments. Let them know *how* you did it.

- ✔ **Divert important questions.** Tickle interviewers' interest by answering most of their questions. Then when asked a particularly important question, you could use it to give them a reason to see you in person. Tell the interviewer that you can better answer that question in person:

  That's an important question — with my skills (experience) in this area, I can cover a bit of ground now but feel I could answer this one more fully in person. Would a face-to-face meeting work for you?

  This strategy will only work if the rapport between you and the interviewer is good and you can be flexible about the meeting time. If you suggest a face-to-face meeting and then have lots of restrictions on when you can meet, all you have done is left an important question unanswered.

- ✔ **Punt the salary question.** Phone screeners often ask you to name an expected salary. Play dodge ball on this one. You don't know how much money you want yet because you don't know what the job is worth. (You find more techniques to avoid premature salary talk in Chapter 7.)

- ✔ **Push for a meeting.** As the call winds to a close, go for the prize:

  As we talk, I'm thinking we can better discuss my qualifications for [position title] in person. I can be flexible but could be at your office Thursday morning. Would this be convenient?

Another statement:

[Interviewer's name], based on the information you've given me, I am very interested in pursuing this work opportunity and would like to schedule a time for us to meet in person. Would that work for you?

When the interviewer agrees but can't set a specific time, simply suggest when you're available and ask when would be a good time to follow up. Remember, what you want is an in-person meeting. Assume you'll get it and give the interviewer a choice as to the time.

✔ **Say thanks.** Express your appreciation for the time spent with you.

✔ **Write a thank you email.** Just because the interview was via phone doesn't negate the wisdom of putting your thanks in an email.

Make your thank you email a sales letter restating the qualifications you bring to the position.

Acing Automated Phone Screens

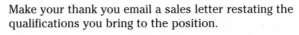

Automated screening interviews, in which you use a phone to answer a fixed list of questions posed by a faceless recorded voice, are used by some recruiters as a time saver. How successful is the technology? The answer depends on whom you ask:

✔ Recruiting professionals say they like automated phone screening because they don't have to play phone tag with candidates, they can schedule blocks of time to listen to all the interviews one after another and forward the best to hiring managers, and they can listen at any hour of the day or night.

✔ Interviewees say they don't like automated phone screening because answering canned questions is cold, rigid and impersonal. They find it uncomfortable to realise that their recorded performances can live on and on and on. They much prefer live, reactive and unscripted responses by someone on the other end of a phone call.

Particulars vary among automated interview vendors, but here's a typical routine: For each position to be filled, the recruiter records up to 12 interview questions. Each question allows a maximum of a two-minute answer.

Nose-to-nose screening

In addition to questionnaires, phones and computers, sometimes you'll score an in-person screening interview, typically at job fairs and shopping malls.

A proactive technique is called the 'job search pop-up' or 'job search ninja' technique — also known as 'cold canvassing'. This involves approaching an employer about work even when the organisation has not advertised.

In the hospitality and retail sector it would involve standing outside stores and restaurants for half an hour before opening time so you can try to talk to managers as they start their day. Your opening pitch is something like this: 'Good morning! I'm [name], a hard-working person seeking a [type of job]. I have exceptional references and useful experience. Can we talk briefly about my working here?'

Automated phone screening systems often work on a 'one-and-done' rule. That is, once you have recorded your answer to a question, you can't rerecord your answer even if you immediately realise that your original answer was weak or wrong. Double-check your understanding of whether the one-and-done rule applies to your interview before you begin recording.

How do you know when you're selected to interview by recording? An employer sends an interview invitation to you by email or includes an 'interview now' button in a website job posting.

To learn more about how to survive an automated phone screener, visit vendor websites. For the names of specific companies providing this type of screener, do an online search for 'automated phone job interviews'.

Pushing the Right Buttons: Computer Screens

Questionnaires and phone screens aren't the only screening game shows in town. Computer-assisted screens are still around, substituting meetings with a PC or app that takes you directly to a screening website, especially for jobs with high turnover, such as food service and retailing. Here's what you can expect keyboard style.

Most computer programs frame questions in a true/false or multiple-choice format, but some ask for an essay response.

A preset time limit for each question is the norm for digital digging, so be ready to keyboard your answers in a timely manner.

Encourage a friend to try a computer interview you plan to take so you can look at the questions before diving in. Make notes of the questions and reflect on your own upcoming responses before you hit the keyboard. Additionally, if you've never participated in a computer-controlled interview, practice on the employers you least want to work for and save the best for last, when you know what you're doing.

After you run through your computer lines, the computer compiles a summary of your answers, which the interviewer uses to decide whether you flunk the first cut or advance to the next round of interviewing.

Newer computer software allows candidates to type in comments they would like to have considered — for example, eagerness to enter or re-enter the workplace, a history of unemployment due to a sick but now recovered family member, an emphasis that you're no stranger to hard work or that you never leave home without enthusiasm. Inject any comment you would have said to a human interviewer.

Screening Survival Skills Are Now a Must-Have

The goal of the screening interview is to land the selection interview. The goal of the selection interview is to land the job.

According to an old rugby truism, you can't win if you don't score, and you can't score if you don't get the ball. Moving beyond screening interviews is all about getting the ball — so you can run with it.

Sticky wicket screening questions

Be sure you're well rehearsed for potential knockout questions that may come by phone or computer:

✔ Are you willing to relocate at your own expense?

✔ Do you have reliable transportation?

✔ Did you graduate from an accredited college?

✔ Do you have reliable childcare arrangements?

✔ Would you consider a commute of more than 25 kilometres?

✔ Are you willing to travel 50 per cent of your work week?

Screening may also include integrity testing. Employers want to know whether you will steal from them or otherwise turn in an ethically challenged performance. Key: Avoid absolutes, like *always* or *never.* Recruiters are not going to believe that you have never lied, even a teensy, tiny white lie. Learn more by browsing online for 'integrity testing for employment'.

Chapter 3

Interviewing via Video

● ●

In This Chapter

▶ Identifying digital roads to video face-time and prepping for your video interview

▶ Working on your execution during video interviews

▶ Staying conscious of posture and facial expressions

● ●

*A*s smaller recruiting staffs face larger numbers of job applications, some employers are turning to video interviews to cut costs when identifying viable candidates. Overall, video technology is still most often used for initial screening, as described in Chapter 2, or for distance meet-ups when the cost of travel is prohibitive. But for lower-level jobs — such as internships, commodity jobs and some technical positions — the online job video may be the entire interviewing package.

The 21st-century transition of the job interviewing process to video screens — one that's evolving minute by minute — adds a whole new layer of techniques you'll want to master for successful job-hunting. This chapter describes the essentials of nailing the video interview, whether it's used as a screening or selection event.

Some selection interviews may be conducted by phone, instead of face-to-face or via video. If preparing for a phone interview, many of the same principles and tips covered in this chapter apply. (Also check out Chapter 2, which offers tips for screening interviews conducted over the phone.)

Winning the Video Interview

When you're targeting a managerial or professional job, a job offer is unlikely to be extended until the candidate and the person with hiring authority have gone nose-to-nose in the same room.

The video look-over, which may include multiple screening interviews, is usually aimed at reducing in-person meetings to a single event. Having said that, remember that nothing is fixed in bronze in today's rapidly developing online video interviewing industry. After a round of phone and video interviews, job offers are occasionally extended to candidates who've never set foot inside the employer's office.

Not all video interviewing models are the same, and some employers may use more than one model. Regardless of the model, interviewing skills are front and centre in a video version. This section describes the most common basic video model, Skype, and video interviewing skills.

Chatting through Skype

You can interview live using Skype, an online phone and video internet service. But you need a computer with an in-built camera or a webcam plus a decent broadband connection.

Skype started in 2003, and its name is short for 'sky peer-to-peer'. Free to use in its basic version, with an easy registration process, Skype is the best-known service of its type. Skype is now the preferred method many employers use to conduct long-distance screening interviews, although a number stick to 'old-fashioned' phone screeners for simplicity. Comments by interviewees who've tried video chat interviewing range from enthusiastic to grumbly:

> *I really liked the video interview a lot better than the phone-based interview — it was a much friendlier and warmer exchange.*

> *A webcam isn't the most flattering piece of technology. It can make you look as attractive as Jason in* Friday the 13th.

Before you make your first screen appearance on the interview scene via video chat on Skype, take the following steps:

- ✔ Download the Skype software a week or two in advance. Cultivate a first-name basis with it. Set up practice training calls with your friends so you'll look comfortable and polished when real interviews come your way.

- ✔ Create a professional username; this isn't the scene to joke around.

- ✔ On the morning of a real interview, conduct a quick test of the technology to ensure that your camera and microphone are working like a charm.

Getting ready to video interview

As with all interviews, don't walk in cold and sit down before a camera unprepared. The following suggestions brief you on what you need to know.

Time limits

Find out whether you're on a clock for the interview. If the interview is scheduled for 30 minutes, consider it a rigid cut-off and don't plan on overtime.

Advance work

Send materials for show-and-tell in advance of the interview, in case the interviewer wants to ask questions about an updated resume or project; you can't slide materials through the screen.

Content review

Review potential questions that you're likely to be asked. (See Chapters 14 to 19 and 21.) Be ready to relate your qualifications to the job's requirements. Memorise examples of accomplishments that illustrate what you can bring to the company.

Note taking

Making a few notes during an in-person interview is flattering to the interviewer. But the jury's still out about whether you should take a notebook to video interviews and jot down points that will help you respond with clarity. The criticism of note taking is that it is more pronounced and disruptive onscreen than it is face-to-face. Others disagree, saying that glancing at your notes may make you seem more conscientious.

On balance, I vote with the note-taking school. I think it's okay to refer to your notes (and resume) and hopefully be seen as a thorough person who covers all the bases.

Technical check

When you're not interviewing at home, arrive 15 to 30 minutes early at the interview site to deal with any technical issues that may arise. Request an overview of the interviewing event and a refresher on the use of the equipment. Ask the technician how loudly you should speak into the mike and how to use the picture-in-picture feature that shows you in action.

When you're using your own video equipment, check your camera angle (set it at eye level) and speakers (place them out of view). Improve the quality of the audio by wearing a lapel microphone, known as a *lavalier* microphone, clipped to your collar or tie rather than relying on the uncertain audio quality of your webcam.

Each morning before a real interview, double-check your internet connections. Arrange to keep the other internet traffic to a minimum during Skype sessions; make sure no-one is surfing, playing online games or watching streaming video in another room (these all compromise the bandwidth you need for Skype).

Appearance

To avoid a contrast issue, you can't go wrong with solid colours that aren't too dark (black) or too light (white, yellow). Blue works well. Although you may see an anything-goes range of colours on high-definition or digital TV, you can't count on the technology for the average computer monitor being that advanced.

Additionally, busy patterns, stripes and plaids distract from your face. Watch TV newsreaders to form your own wardrobe preferences. Otherwise, wear the clothing you would wear to a same-room interview (see Chapter 8).

Background

Plan for an uncluttered look behind you. Eliminate such distractions as too many books or magazines, wall hangings, memos taped to the wall, stacks of laundry or posters from your favourite band. Avoid background motion — second hands ticking on a clock, barking dogs racing back and forth, cats leaping into camera range, or kids walking in and out of camera range, for instance.

Lighting

Eliminate any bright light (as from a window) behind you — it will darken your face.

Dress rehearsal

Arrange test interviews with friends. Can you hear each other? Can you see each other? Is the framing of your screen about right (head to waist), or is the focus on your face so tight that every pore looks like a moon crater?

Go beyond merely conducting test interviews with friends — record your performances to see for yourself how you're coming across on camera. In addition to paying attention to the quality of your answers and how you look overall, be on the lookout for awkward or off-putting behaviours, such as the following actions:

- Swinging your leg
- Tapping your foot
- Fiddling with your hair
- Leaning back
- Crossing your arms
- Looking dour
- Slumping or slouching
- Reacting in slow motion

Recording and watching yourself, more than any other tip, will improve your interviewing performance.

Rock the Video Job Interview

The *content* of a video interview is much the same as an in-person interview. But the *execution* differs. Consider these sample reactions:

✔ A candidate, a cool 20-something manager who isn't easily thrown off centre, told a magazine that his video interview was 'kind of nerve-wracking' and a totally different feeling from sitting in front of someone for a live interview.

✔ An employer reported on a comments board that many things don't come across on camera and that certain factors are accentuated: 'Posture, dress, comfort with uncertainty, facility with technology — all those things get highlighted and bolded during a web interview.'

Online, you can't use handshakes and ingratiating small talk as you enter and leave an interviewer's office to help imprint favourable memories of you. To compensate, include a memorable statement — a sound bite. Somewhere near the end of the interview, an experienced candidate says something like this:

> *Of the things I've accomplished in my career, [name a top achievement] stands out as the most significant. Do you see a strong connection between my favourite accomplishment and what it will take to be very successful in this position?*

An entry-level candidate can aim to become unforgettable by saying something unexpected like this:

> *I know that many employers consider my generation to be lacking in writing and critical thinking skills and aren't pleased that some of us write company email as if we were texting mobile-phone messages with our thumbs. That's not me. I'm good with technology, but I'm old fashioned. I spell my words correctly and include all the letters. And I believe you will be happy to know that I use my head when I write — not just my thumb. I hope we can get together and speak face-to-face soon.*

During the Interview

You're almost prepared to command the screen. Now review the finer points provided in this section, gleaned from others who have gone in front of the cameras before you.

Movements and posture

Calmness is classy and shows confidence. By no means should you check your personality at the door, but do try to be fairly still. Smooooth. Avoid overly broad gestures — you're not directing traffic. Ration your gestures to underscore important information.

Pause and think before answering a question, to seem thoughtful and unflappable.

Look interested when you're seated by leaning slightly forward with the small of your back against your chair.

Microphones have an irritating habit of picking up all the noise in the room. Don't shuffle papers or tap a pen. Noises that you may not notice in a same-room interview can become annoying in a video interview.

Occasionally glance at the picture-in-picture feature on the monitor to check your body language — and hope you don't catch yourself scratching, licking your lips or jangling your keys. Hunching your shoulders and other bad-posture poses make you look even worse on those small screens than they do in person.

Facial expressions and speaking

The first thing you say is, 'Hi, I'm Bill Kennedy. Nice to meet you.' (And if you're not Bill Kennedy, use your own name.) Speak normally, but not too fast. When nervous, some people don't stop for air, and their best lines are lost, unheard or not understood.

Be conscious of a sound delay. A couple of seconds will lapse between when the interviewer speaks and when you hear the statement or question (you observe this audio pause on TV when a foreign correspondent is on another continent). At the end of an interviewer's words, pause for a second or two before you reply.

Look directly at the camera as often as possible when speaking — this is how you make eye contact. You can look around occasionally, but avoid rolling your eyes all over the room as though you can hardly wait to make your getaway. Some people look down at the desk. Don't, especially if you have a bald, shiny spot on the top of your dome. And don't bend over a microphone; imagine that the interviewer is sitting across the table from you. (If available, remember to use a lavalier microphone and eliminate that temptation.)

The three most important things to remember in a video interview are (1) smile, (2) smile and (3) smile. Have you noticed that, even when reporting disasters of nationwide proportions, TV newsreaders don't always wipe the smile off their faces? Why do you suppose that is? Smile!

Virtual handshake

Unless your interview space is on fire, ending the interview isn't your prerogative. Always allow the interviewer to indicate when time's up.

Since you can't shake hands through a monitor, deliver a sign-off statement indicating you understand that the interview is over. You can say something as simple as, 'Thank you for your time today. I enjoyed hearing about the role and the company. I hope we can talk face-to-face very soon.'

For other sign-off ideas, review Chapter 11. When you're in a professional setting, push the mute button and leave the room. When you're at home, mute the mike and close the camera.

Learn about videos by viewing videos

A number of free online videos present show-and-tells on the details of delivering a golden performance in the interviewing arena. Get yourself started by browsing for 'How to Ace a Job Interview on Skype,' by Barbara Kiviat for Time.com. The staging directions alone are worth the look.

Chapter 4

Preparing for Different Types of Interviews

*Y*ou know the old saying: 'Variety is the spice of life'. (Yes, you can groan now.)

Variety, in today's job market, is also rich in job interviewing dramas. Do yourself a favour by becoming familiar with the various shapes, forms and fashions job interviews take in today's employment market.

This chapter helps you accomplish just that as it highlights the most common styles of job interviews. For convenience, I divide them into four clusters, describing the

✔ *Objective* for the interview

✔ *Interviewer number*, from one to many

✔ *Technique and interview forms* that shape your participation

✔ *Location* where the interview takes place

Mastering Interviews by Objective

Interviewers set up different kinds of meetings for different reasons, just like you have different objectives when meeting friends or family. Sometimes you're happy to meet up with your extended family and let them ramble on about what everyone has been up to, and sometimes you want to cut straight to the chase and find out exactly what happened at last year's Christmas party.

The upcoming sections are all about interview objectives.

Screening interview

Interviewing is a two-stage process in large organisations. The two stages are *screening* and *selection*. Screening precedes selection.

The purpose of screening — or first-cut interviews — is to weed out all applicants except the best qualified.

Live (in-person) interviews to screen applicants typically are held at the employer's worksite, recruitment firms and employment services, university and college career services and job fairs.

But interviewers increasingly rely on technology — such as telephone, online and webcam interviews — to screen applicants. They use the technology as a cost-cutting move to knock out underskilled, overskilled, wrong fit or overpriced candidates before their companies invest too much time and money in dead ends.

The *screener*, usually an employee of the organisation from inside the human resources department or a consultant engaged from an outside recruitment firm, quizzes all comers and passes the short-listed candidates to the person who makes the final selection.

The *selector* — that is, the person who has the final say on hiring — is usually the department manager or the boss to whom the victorious candidate will report.

Recruiter general screening interview

Contingency recruiters get paid only when they find a candidate to fill a vacant job role. More than one recruitment company could be vying to fill a particular role on a contingency basis.

The more people contingency recruiters see, the larger the candidate pool they have to choose from when trying to fill a particular role. Getting an interview with a contingency recruiter or employment agency consultant is easier than with a retained recruiter because they may view you as a possible candidate for roles they have not yet advertised or for a client they hope to bring on board. But you still can't waste a contingency recruiter's time. Hand over your resume and give your best performance to show a broad selection of work experiences. You're trying to make the contingency recruiter remember you for a variety of future job openings.

An employer could also engage a recruitment firm on a *retainer* basis. Retained firms operate on an exclusive basis to fill a vacant job for their client — the employer. The retained firm usually charge an up-front fee and they work closely with the client — and may have worked for the client for many years — and so know the organisation very well. They're not looking to find a large number of possible candidates but a select number of strong candidates.

Whether you are dealing with a contingency or retained recruiter, take care to score well in the following qualities:

- ✔ Competence in skills and knowledge
- ✔ Enthusiasm and motivated interest in work
- ✔ Experience (some job history)
- ✔ Good communication
- ✔ Leadership and initiative
- ✔ Personality/likeability

Recruiter search interview

A recruiter will contact you either because you've applied for a job in response to a job advertisement, you've posted your resume on the recruitment firm's website or the consultant has found you via referral or a professional profile that you have posted online through a site such as LinkedIn.

So when a recruiter contacts you about a specific job opening, chances are the reason is that you've done or are doing a job similar to the one the recruiter's client wants to fill. You may not be told the name of the client (employer) at first but the recruiter believes you already know the basics of your industry and the role available and can hit the ground running if hired.

The recruiter is prepared for the (de facto screening) interview on first contact; you're not. When contacted by a recruiter, level the playing field by saying you were walking out the door for an important appointment and schedule the interview for the following day — this gives you the chance to gather a few basic facts about the opportunity to help you prepare.

Recruiters — whether third-party or internal — can't hire you, but they're nonetheless the gatekeepers to a great many jobs. If you don't impress the recruiter, chances are you won't get to meet the employer. Whenever you're dealing with recruiters, you need to deliver a great performance.

To impress a recruiter in a search interview:

✔ Show that you have definite career goals and indicate how this position fits those goals.

✔ Even though you may not know the name of the employer, ask probing, thoughtful questions about the type of company looking to hire and the role on offer. If you do know the name of the company hiring, you can ask even more detailed questions about the employer's priorities and challenges to show you have done your homework.

You don't have to wait for a recruitment firm to contact you. Use the web to research recruitment firms that specialise in your industry or occupation. Start with the following resources:

✔ Australian Recruiter (www.australianrecruiter. com.au) allows you to search for recruiters based on your profession. Simply use the tag cloud to browse agencies by the professions into which they recruit, or use the Keyword and Category Search boxes to be more specific with your search if you're targeting a niche profession.

✔ The Australian Employment Guide (employmentguide. com.au) is a free service, with content provided by leading recruiters, HR and career management experts. Under the 'Recruitment Agencies' tab, you can find information about Australia's top 10 agencies, based on coverage.

✔ Careers NZ (www.careers.govt.nz) not only lists general NZ recruitment agencies, but also provides a comprehensive list of industry-specific recruiters. From the home page, go to the 'How to Get a Job' tab and click on 'Job Vacancy and Recruitment Websites'.

Selection interview with an employer

The selection interview (sometimes called the decision interview) is typically a live interview (face-to-face). You meet with a supervisor, department head or another person who has the authority to hire you. (Sometimes the selection decision is made by more than one person, as I explain in the later section 'Group interview'.)

Because this final interviewer will be your potential boss, you should see the interview as a two-way process. You should use the interview to evaluate the interviewer and the organisation to ensure the job opportunity is right for you.

Selection interviewers are rarely pros at interviewing and often just go with their intuition, hoping the task is over as quickly as possible so that they can get back to their 'real' work. Often, however, an internal HR professional will be sitting in on the interview with your potential boss to ensure formal questions are asked and to test if you are a cultural fit for the organisation. Treat both interviewers with equal respect.

Because the selection interview may take several detours, be ready to ask leading questions to (1) get the interview back on track and (2) set up an opening to describe your qualifications for the position.

Even if the questioner seems like a long-lost buddy, don't relax. Your interviewer is trying to decide which candidate is the best investment for the company. A wrong choice can cost the company thousands of dollars in training time, in correcting any mistakes made and in terminating the person's employment. Plus the organisation would need to start the hiring process again.

Selection interviewers are looking for

- ✔ **Strong presentation of personality:** How you blend with other employees, as well as your general likeability and motivation to work

- ✔ **Specific details of your competencies and skills:** How your qualifications allow you to do the job better than other candidates

✔ **Specific details of your job experience or education:** Not only how you've been trained to do a similar job but also how you have performed in that job — and how you'll apply that background to the new job

✔ **How you handle specific job scenarios:** How your mind works under variable or stressful conditions, and how you solve challenges

Assuming that the person conducting the interview will be your boss or a colleague with whom you have to get along, the selection interview is where you move from neutral behaviour into high gear. This is the forum where you reveal the best of your workplace personality!

The selection interview is also where you take note of how you and your potential boss blend. If your gut instinct tells you the blend is oil-and-water, think twice before saying 'yes' to this job if it's offered.

Even when every other factor about the job is tempting, your work life will be a happier place when you and your future boss are 'using the same software'.

Combination interview

Small firms often combine the screening and selection interviews. The resulting combination can be short if the interviews are conducted by the owner of a small business or long and arduous if conducted by a professional recruitment firm or HR consultant. If long and involved, the process not only tests your match to the hiring requirements, but also measures your stamina and motivation for the job.

From the very first exchange, pull out all the stops in selling your top qualities and displaying a pleasant personality, because you won't get a second chance.

Interviewing for internal promotion

Moving up from the inside as an internal candidate often is easier than gaining access as an outside candidate. But it's not a sure thing.

Approach a promotion interview as though you were heading out to a new company. Research diligently, as I describe in Chapter 5, to be able to talk about industry trends and other big issues.

When you're the only insider wrangling for the job, use your knowledge of the company's policies, plans and culture to emphasise that you alone can hit the floor running — which no outsider can actually do. Then identify several current company problems you could deal with right off the bat.

Be cautious about suggesting solutions to company problems caused by the person interviewing you or by others within their team or department. When in doubt, don't point out problems. Wait until you're asked how you would solve a particular issue and even then be tactful.

Should you emphasise your 20 years of loyal service with a show-and-tell of your successes at a time when your company is handing off generational control from boomers to Xers or Gen Ys? Although it may seem counterintuitive to older candidates, if that's you, tread carefully. The familiar 'tried-and-proven' strategy won't have legs during a time when new captains are determined to justify taking the wheel by steering in different directions.

A youth-oriented management doesn't care about the glories of Ancient Rome or Ancient You — what they care about is whether you can do the work ahead, now and tomorrow.

So while you can include the accomplishments of the past ten years (no more than that), also reframe the discussion to focus on work samples and skills that highlight your ability to do the new job. Give examples of your flexible personality. Identify times when you welcomed new tasks and responsibilities. Help them see you as the way forward, not as someone stuck in days long gone.

Second interviews and beyond

Being called back is a good sign: You're a few steps closer to being offered the job you want.

To come out on top in the second interview, be sure you understand the dynamics at play. (Actually, the second interview may turn out to be a series of interviews, but the purpose is typically the same in all of them.)

Interviewing for a government job

The public sector of Australia and New Zealand offer a large range of employment opportunities, and public sector interviews usually follow a similar and set script.

If your application for a position in the Australian public service is short-listed, a selection team or a panel may interview you. Key selection criteria would have been used to evaluate your application, and these criteria will also influence the kinds of questions you'll be asked in the interview, as the selection team tries to get a better understanding of your skills and abilities.

Questions could include behavioural-based questions, and hypothetical scenario questions. You may also be asked to do exercises such as a work sample test (refer to Chapter 1

for more on this), presentations or psychometric testing (see Chapter 6).

In New Zealand, government organisations usually allow candidates to bring a *Whanau* (a Maori word for 'extended family') or support group or person to their interview, if they wish. This gives candidates personal support and lets others speak of their merits, when it is culturally inappropriate or difficult for them to do so themselves.

Whether applying for a government job in Australia or New Zealand, you can greatly improve your chances by looking at the agency website and reading any publicly available information about the agency, so you have a strong understanding of what they do. Also look for the agency's most recent annual report, and even their corporate plan.

Here, I describe three kinds of second interviews and suggest tips to come out ahead in each one:

- ✔ **The 'yours-to-lose' selection interview:** The decision is virtually made in your favour. But the hiring manager is confirming it with endorsements and buy-in consensus from the team. Your qualifications aren't in question, but your fit (how you fit in with the company culture) is being probed. Relax a little — these are your new colleagues. Keep your answers pleasant, straightforward and brief but not terse.

- ✔ **The finalists' selection interview:** The decision has narrowed to two or three finalists. Keep selling your qualifications. Allude to cultural fit with subtle comments suggesting that you're one of them. ('I agree that we must build adequate electrical power into the infrastructure.') Ask intelligent questions, such as depth of support for stated missions and professional development opportunities.

✔ **The 'do-over' screening interview:** Management still wonders whether you're underqualified and overpriced and wants to make another pass at you, perhaps with different screeners. Expect questions all over again about your job history, skills, salary history or requirements, resume gaps and the kind of person you are. (You're reliable, honest, team-oriented and, overall, have laudable values.) Never show impatience with being asked the same questions again. Treat the interview as a fresh opportunity to shine.

If you're working with a recruiter, ask the recruiter for tips about what more you can do to demonstrate you're the right person for the job. Also, ask the recruiter about where you are in the selection process. If you're not dealing with a recruiter, ask the same questions of the interviewer who has shown you the greatest interest.

Why offers don't follow interviews

When you've been through three, four, five, six or more interviews for the job that ultimately went to another person, suspect any of the following reasons:

✔ Oh my, while you were an outstanding candidate, someone else was even more perfect for the role. The decision could have been a very close call.

✔ Your image doesn't reflect the role you seek to play (see Chapter 8).

✔ Your referees are failing to meet your expectations of high praise (see Chapter 11).

✔ You're asking for a bigger pay packet than your performance supports (see Chapter 7).

✔ Someone on the 'panel of judges' voted you off the show, and you may never know who the sneak is.

✔ The interviewing flurry was a dodge to cover up the real script — the job was always going to go to a friend, relative or internal applicant.

Mastering Interviews by Interviewer

The most common interview style you'll encounter is the one in which a solo interviewer meets and questions you. Another possibility is that you'll meet face to face with several pairs of measuring eyes — all at once. Still another format shuffles you from one interview to another to another, all within the same company. In the following sections, I sketch the possibilities.

One-to-one interview

You and the employer meet, usually at the employer's office, and discuss the job and your relevant skills and other qualifications that relate to it. You find suggestions on how to take victory laps in the one-to-one interview format throughout this book.

Group interview

The plot thickens. Also called a panel, board, team, collective or committee interview, this style puts you centre stage before a crowd — anywhere from three questioners up. Usually they're people from the department where you would work, or they may come from various departments throughout the organisation.

You wouldn't be at this expensive meeting (think of all the salaries for the group's time) if you hadn't already been pre-screened to establish your qualifications match the role. These people are gathered to see whether they like you and whether you'll fit into their operation. Greet and make eye contact with each person. Appear confident. Make a quick seating chart to help you remember names.

Before you answer a first question, smile, thank everyone for inviting you to meet with them, and then begin your answer, which will probably be 'You asked me to tell you about myself ...'

Should you try to identify the leader and direct most of your remarks to that person? No. The boss may be the quiet observer in the corner. Play it safe — maintain eye contact with all committee members. When starting to answer a question, look first at the person who posed the question but then shift eye contact to direct your answer to the leader and then all panel members. In this performance, play to everyone in the room!

Group interviews highlight your interpersonal skills, leadership and ability to think on your feet and deal with issues in a stressful setting. The purpose of a group interview is not only to hear what you say, but also to see what behaviours and skills you display within a group.

When the interview is over, thank the group as though you just finished a speech.

> *Thank you for having me here today. I enjoyed being with you. This interview confirmed my research indicating that this organisation is a good place to work. I'll look forward to hearing from you and, hopefully, joining you.*

While making eye contact with your audience is critical during a job interview, don't be put off if those judging your performance don't respond in the same way. Panel interviews, particularly for public service roles, often require those listening to your answers to mark off a form or make specific notes so heads may be buried while you're talking.

Ask questions. Periodically summarise important points to keep the group focused. Use a notebook to record several simultaneous questions, explaining that you don't want to omit responding to anyone's important concern.

Serial interview

A serial interview also involves a group of people, but not all at once. You're handed off from person to person. Typically, you're passed from screener to line manager to top manager — and perhaps a half-dozen people in between in the drawn-out process of the serial interview. You strengthen your chances each time you're passed onward.

Use your screening (plain vanilla personality) interview behaviour with all interviewers you meet except those with whom you would work. Then go into your selection (full personality) mode.

Brainteaser job interview

Brainteasers in a job interview ('Why are manhole covers round?', 'How would you test a salt shaker?', 'Which state would you eliminate from Australia and why?') may be used to challenge candidates to see who can rise and shine through the ranks in today's hypercompetitive work environment.

When you suspect that you're heading into interview combat, find guidance in a book by John Kador, business-writing consultant (www.jkador.com). *How to Ace the Brain Teaser Interview* (McGraw-Hill) is a smart book on logic-driven riddles and oxygen-sucking puzzles that job interviewers may spring on you without warning.

When the initial interviewer says that you're being passed on to the second interviewer, try to find out a little about the second interviewer. Ask a question like, 'What role does [name of second interviewer] play in the organisation? Do they feel the same way about customer service as you do?' You'll get the information you need to establish common ground with your next interviewer. Continue the advance-tip technique all the way to the finish line.

When you're interviewed by one person after another, consistency counts. Don't tell a rainbow of stories about the same black-and-white topics. When interview team members later compare notes, they should be discussing the same person.

Mastering Interviews by Technique

A job interviewer bears the responsibility for the hiring of a particular candidate — and when that candidate disappoints, no-one's happy.

A film director calls the shots on a movie set, placing actors and cameras to best advantage. Similarly, a job interviewer sets the technique and tone of the interview, whether it's behaviour-based, tightly or loosely controlled, intentionally stressful, or loaded with brain-crunching puzzles.

Behaviour-based interview

Behaviour-based interviewing relies on storytelling — examples of what you've done that support your claims. Premised on the belief that your past behaviour is a predictor of your future behaviour, this style of interviewing is used to quiz candidates about how they have handled specific situations in past roles. Behaviour-based interviewing emphasises 'What *did* you do back when?' instead of 'What *would* you do if?' The interviewer wants to know the kinds of behaviours you have used before to solve problems.

The presumption is that if you were a good problem solver in the past, you'll be a good problem solver in the future. Interview questions are designed to draw out clues to a candidate's workplace DNA. All candidates are asked virtually the same questions. The tip-off that you've just been handed a behaviour-based question is when the question begins with words such as:

- ✔ Tell me about a time when —
- ✔ Give me an example of your skills in —
- ✔ Describe a time when you —
- ✔ Why did you —

 Use 'I' statements instead of 'we' statements when recalling examples of past performance. If you did work on a project or solution with a team, you can mention that but be clear about detailing the particular role you played.

A few fleshed-out examples illustrate the behaviour-based technique more fully:

> *Think back to a time when you were on the verge of making a huge sale, and the customer baulked at the last minute, promised to get back to you, but didn't. What action did you take?*

> *Tell me about an on-the-job disaster that you turned around, making lemonade from lemons.*

> *Describe the types of risks you have allowed your direct reports to take.*

> *Can you give me an example of when you were able to implement a vision for your organisation?*

Recall the last time you worked with a difficult colleague. How were you able to establish a good working relationship?

Why did you decide to major in sociology at Melbourne University instead of one closer to home?

Companies using behaviour-based interviewing first must identify the behaviours important to the job. If leadership, for instance, is one of the valued behaviours, several questions asking for stories of demonstrated leadership will be asked:

Tell me about the last time you had to take charge of a project but were lacking in clear direction. How did you carry the project forward?

Because the behavioural style of interviewing attempts to measure predictable behaviour rather than pure paid work experience, it can help level the playing field for rookies competing against seasoned candidates.

In mining your past for anecdotes, you can draw from virtually any part of your past behaviour — education, school projects, paid work experience, volunteer work, activities, hobbies or family life.

As you sift through your memories, be on the lookout for a theme; the motif that runs through your choices of education, jobs and activities. Put at least half a dozen anecdotes that illustrate your theme in your mental pocket and pull them out when you need them. Examples of themes are

- ✔ Displaying leadership
- ✔ Solving problems
- ✔ Negotiating
- ✔ Showing initiative
- ✔ Overcoming adversity
- ✔ Succeeding
- ✔ Dealing with stress
- ✔ Sacrificing to achieve an important work goal
- ✔ Dealing with someone who disagreed with you

- ✔ Displaying commitment
- ✔ Demonstrating a work ethic
- ✔ Staying task orientated
- ✔ Practising communication skills

Here are several more suggestions to skate your way through behaviour-based questions:

- ✔ Tell a story with a beginning, a middle and an end using the PAR technique — problem, action, result.

  Here's an example. *Problem:* An e-commerce company was operating at a substantial loss. *Action:* I outsourced technical support and added seven new product lines. *Result:* We cut our expenses by 8 per cent, increased our revenues by 14 per cent and had our first profitable year, with expectations of higher profits next year.

- ✔ If you're a rookie, don't simply cite the subject of your classes — 'I couldn't solve my accounting problem, so I asked my lecturer.' No! Look back at your student class projects, previous work experience, and extracurricular activities. Reach into real life for your success stories.

- ✔ Try not to sound as though you memorised every syllable and inflection, or like a machine with all the answers. Admitting that your example was a complex problem and that you experimented until you found its best solution humanises you.

- ✔ Be prepared to be asked about a time when you made a mistake or failed, and what you learned from the experience. Don't be defensive. No-one is perfect and the employer or recruiter is probing to see how well you bounce back from setbacks.

The interviewer is more interested in the process than in the details of your success stories. What was the reasoning behind your actions? Why did you behave the way you did? What skills did you use?

Behaviour-based interviewing, which arrived nearly 50 years ago, is popular today because employers are trying to snatch clues from history to predict the future. The underlying rationale is that people tend to play the same roles in life over and over.

Directive interview

The *directive interview* is one in which the interviewer maintains complete control and walks you through the discussion to uncover what the interviewer wants to know.

The *structured* interview is directive because the interviewer works from a written list of questions asked of all candidates and writes down your answers.

The argument in favour of structured interviews is that they promote fairness, uncover superior candidates and eliminate the cloning effect (in which an interviewer essentially hires candidates in her own image — or one who the interviewer thinks will 'fit in' merely because of shared values).

In structured interviews, the interviewer may throw out a *critical incident* and ask you to respond. A critical incident is a specific problem or challenge that was successfully handled by employees of the company. Like a quiz show, the host (the interviewer) has the 'answer sheet' — the actual behaviour that solved the problem or met the challenge.

Some critical incidents can be anticipated by researching industry trends and inferred by reading company press releases online.

Whether you're in an unwritten directive interview or a scripted structured interview, expect interviewers to ask both closed- and open-ended questions.

A *closed-ended question* can be answered with *yes* or *no*:

> *Did you find my office easily?*

An *open-ended question* usually asks *how* or *why*:

> *How do you like this industry?*

This interviewer has an agenda and is intent on seeing that it's followed. Being too assertive in changing the topic is a mistake. The only safe way you can introduce one of your skills is to ask a relevant question that helps you guide the interview onto safer ground:

> *Would you like to hear about my experience in XYZ [a specific area of the industry where you have lots of knowledge]?*

Nondirective interview

A *nondirective interview* rewards you for leading the discussion. It's often an approach of line managers who don't know much about professional interviewing.

Questions tend to be broad and general so that you can elaborate and tell all kinds of terrific stories about yourself. A few questions may reveal key areas of the employer's needs. These questions may sound at first as though they're critical incidents, but in this loose-limbed interview, the interviewer probably doesn't assume that he or she knows the answers. Examples of nondirective interview questions include the following:

> *We had a problem employee last quarter who revealed information about our marketing strategies to a competitor — how would you handle this situation?*

> *You understand some of the difficulties this department faces — how would you approach these in your first four months?*

> *Tell me about your goals in the next five years and how this position fits in with them.*

> *Your resume shows you can speak Chinese and have a degree in computer science — how do you plan to use both of these skills in this position?*

 Carry agenda cards or a small notebook with a list of your qualifications and a list of questions about the company. When you have to carry the ball, working from notes can be a lifesaver if you have a leaky memory.

If all your preparation fails you, fall back on how you would find a solution and then engage the interviewer — for example, 'I wish I had the answer. If faced with such an issue I would [describe the action you would take]. What's your viewpoint on this?'

Stress interview

Recognising that hazing goes on in a stress interview is important. Recognise it for what it is — either it's a genuine test of your ability to do the job, or the interviewer is being deliberately provocative and could be a certified jerk.

Storytelling your way to a job

Prepare for all your interviews — not just behaviour-based interviews — by recalling anecdotes from your past experience that back up your claims of skills and other qualifications. Work on these stories and rehearse them as though you're going to present them in a speech before hundreds of people. Make them fun, interesting — even exciting! Few of us are natural-born storytellers, but do your best to tell a good story.

Experts claim the way to breeze through behaviour-based interviews is to prepare, rehearse and deliver one to two minute stories about your skills, experience and accomplishments that relate directly to the job. Your commitment to meeting interviewers' interests shows as you recognise their goals and pay your respects in full with relevant stories.

Whichever it is, don't take the horrors of a stress interview — also called a *confrontational* interview — personally. Keep your cool and play the game if you want the job. Don't sweat. Don't cry. Your most reliable tactic is to speak with calm, unflagging confidence. You may have to practise remaining poised in the face of an interviewer's intimidation tactics.

Suppose that you're in sales. Asking you to sell the interviewer something — like the office chair — is fairly common. But having you face blinding sunlight while sitting in a chair with one short leg is, at best, immature.

Stress interviews often consist of

- Hour-long waits before the interview
- Long, uncomfortable silences
- Challenges of your beliefs
- A brusque interviewer or multiple curt interviewers
- Deliberate misinterpretation of your comments and outright insults

Typical questions run along these lines:

Why weren't you working for so long?

Why eight jobs in ten years?

*Your resume shows that you were with your last company
for a number of years without promotion and a virtually flat
salary; why is that?*

*Can you describe a situation when your work was criticised
or you disliked your boss?*

Would you like to have my job?

What would you do if violence erupted in your workplace?

A famous admiral, now dead, used to nail the furniture to the
floor and ask the applicant to pull up a chair. If an interviewer
crosses your personal line of reasonable business behaviour,
stand up with dignity, thank the interviewer for their time and
run like hell for the emergency exit.

Mastering Interviews at Different Locations

Australia and New Zealand have some pretty different — and
wild — locations, where you may have to deal with snakes,
poisonous spiders, freezing cold or searing heat. But hopefully
you can save these sorts of locations for your breaks from work,
not your interviews.

While not every interview takes place across a desk at the
company's home base, presumably you won't have to worry
about snakes or spiders as you head out for an interview over a
meal, in a campus interviewing room or at a job fair.

Mealtime interview

Just when you thought you'd been through all the interviewing
hoops and assumed that landing the job was a done deal, you
get a luncheon invitation from a higher-up in the company,
perhaps your potential boss. Why?

Robin Jay, author of *The Art of the Business Lunch: Building
Relationships Between 12 and 2* (Career Press), identifies the
following reasons:

- ✔ To judge you on your social skills and manners
- ✔ To find out additional information about you that an
  employer may not legally be able to ask

✔ To get to know you better

✔ To compare your social behaviour to that of other candidates

As an account executive, Jay ate her way through 3,000 business lunches. (No, she doesn't now avoid eating in the middle of the day.) She says that sharing a meal with someone reveals her personality faster and more effectively than all the office interviews in the world. 'Many a job has been won or lost at the table,' Jay observes.

So while a mealtime interview may seem more relaxed and social, stay as alert as you would in any other location. Mealtime interviewers are watching you with big eyes.

To avoid spilling precious job opportunities, mind your manners:

✔ Don't order meals so hard to eat that you spend the entire interview lost in your plate with long pasta or saucy, messy or bony food.

✔ Don't order alcohol unless you're at dinner and the person interviewing does so — even then, have only one drink. White wine is a good choice.

✔ Don't order the most expensive or the most inexpensive thing on the menu.

✔ Don't smoke, even if in a smoking area (companies are concerned about employee health and associated time off work).

✔ Don't complain about anything — the food, the service or the restaurant.

✔ Don't over-order or leave too much food on your plate.

To look classy in a mealtime interview, be sure to

✔ Order something that's easy to eat (like a club or veggie sandwich).

✔ Chew with your mouth closed, speak with your mouth empty. Take small bites to ensure you don't keep an interviewer waiting a long time while you finish chewing and swallowing before answering a question.

✔ Order something similar to what the interviewer orders or ask the interviewer to suggest something.

✔ Show your appreciation for the treat — once hired, you may find yourself bringing your lunch in most days.

Practise a technique known as *mirroring* — what the boss or the interviewer does, you do. Take the interviewer's lead in where to rest arms on the table, which fork to hold and how fast to shovel in the food. Subconsciously, you're establishing similarities, making the interviewer like you. (See the sidebar 'Bravo moves for all interviewing styles', later in this chapter.)

Always be polite to the restaurant staff, even if the service or food is so bad you make a mental note never to set foot in the place again. Treating the wait staff with disrespect is worse than spilling spaghetti sauce all over the interviewer's new suit.

No matter how much or how little the tab, the interviewer always pays, so don't reach for the bill when it comes, even if it's placed closer to you. Let it sit there unclaimed, unloved. Remember, this could be a test of your confidence or of your knowledge of protocol.

On-campus interview

Some employers recruit on campuses by setting up interviews through your university's career centre or by making special presentations. These are screening interviews conducted by company recruiters. (Check out the earlier section in this chapter titled 'Screening interview,' and also refer to Chapter 2.)

My tip for university and training college leavers: Snag the interviews you want by learning and using the system. Sign up for resume and job interviewing workshops, make friends with the career centre counsellors, and ask for job leads.

When you don't get the interview slots you want, check back for last-minute cancellations or additions to the interview schedules.

Job fair interview

Job fairs are brief but significant encounters in which you hand over documents — either your resume or a summary sheet of your qualifications (carry both types of documents). Your objective is to land an interview, not get a job offer on the spot at the fair. At best, you'll get a screening interview at the event site.

Try to pre-register for the job fair, get a list of participating employers and research those you plan to visit. Your edge is to be better prepared than the competition.

Lines at career fairs can be long, so accept the likelihood that you'll be standing in many of them. Make use of your time by writing up notes from one recruiter while standing in line to meet another.

Everyone tries to arrive early, so think about arriving at half-time when the first flood has subsided. Dress professionally, whatever that means in your career field.

Work up a branding brief (see Chapter 14) with at least one strong memorable point to say to recruiters. Here's an example: *I am in the top 1 per cent of my environmental engineering class.* If you don't get immediate feedback inviting you for an interview, hand over your summary sheet and ask, 'Do you have positions appropriate for my background?' If the answer is positive, your next question is 'I'd like to take the next step — can we set up an interview?' If you don't get a positive response, continue with 'Can we talk on the phone next week?'

Whether or not you're able to schedule an interview on the spot, when you leave, hand over your resume. Think of your job fair interaction with recruiters as a major star's cameo performance in a film: Move in, make a high-profile impression through dress and preparedness, and move on to the next prospect.

Bravo moves for all interviewing styles

No matter what style of interview you're doing, some factors are all-purpose job winners.

🗸 **Make them like you.** No matter how scientific the interviewing style, the quality of likeability is a powerful influence in deciding who gets the job. And it's human nature to like people who like us, and who are like us in common interests and outlooks.

Show your similarities to the interviewer and company culture. You need not be clones of each other, but do find areas of mutual interest: Preferences in movies, methods of doing work or favourite company products, for instance. When you successfully intimate that you and the decision-making interviewer share similar worldviews, values or approaches to work, you create affinity that leads to job offers.

🗸 **Listen well to interviewers' questions, statements, and feelings.** People like to be listened to more than they like to listen. Show your likeability by summarising, rephrasing and playing back what interviewers say instead of concentrating just on what you have to say.

🗸 **Don't drip honey by overdoing compliments or small talk.** Take cues from the interviewer's office mementos just long enough to break the ice. Most interviewers will be turned off by such transparent plays for empty approval. Get to the point — the job.

🗸 **Pause thoughtfully.** Show that you think as you talk. It's okay to pause in thoughtfulness during an in-person interview, where interviewers can tell you're contemplating and thinking things through before answering. Exception: Don't take a thinking pause during a telephone or videoconferencing interview, where any pause is dead airtime.

🗸 **Take notes.** Have a small notebook handy and use it when the interviewer is talking, especially after you've asked a question or the interviewer has put special emphasis on a subject. Taking notes not only shows that you're paying attention, but also flatters the interviewer. If you prefer to use a laptop or tablet to take notes, ask first: 'May I make a few notes as we talk? I don't want to forget any of your key points.'

Part II

The Power of Researching and Rehearsing

Five Topics to Focus on When Asking Questions in Interviews

- ✔ **The job itself:** Sell yourself by asking questions that are work focused, task focused and function focused. For example, *What percentage of time would I spend communicating with customers?*

- ✔ **The position's duties and challenges:** For example, ask, *What would my key responsibilities be? What results would you expect from my efforts and on what timetable?*

- ✔ **The outcomes you're expected to produce:** For example, *What would be my first project if I were hired for this position? What resources would I have to do the job?*

- ✔ **Where the position sits in the company:** Find out how the position fits into the department and the department into the company.

- ✔ **Typical assignments:** For example, *Can you describe a typical day? Would on-the-job training be required for a new product?*

Check out a free online article about crosscultural interviewing at www.dummies.com/extras/successfuljobinterviewsau.

In this part...

- Research companies and job positions, and rehearse your interviewing style to ensure you present your fully prepared best self.

- Work your way through personality tests and handle salary talk.

- Dress the part and ensure your choice of outfit is appropriate for the type of job you're interviewing for.

- Make a good impression with the questions you ask and with your parting pitch, and analyse your performance after the interview.

Chapter 5

Research Is Your Ticket to Success

*E*ven if you'd rather scrub floors than do quiz-show-quality research on organisations and their people, suck it up and dig right in. Consider the rewards:

✔ You'll have solid facts demonstrating harmony between your qualifications and the job's requirements.

✔ You'll grab data suggesting you're a good fit with an employer's organisational culture.

✔ You'll have the ammo for brilliant answers when asked, 'What do you know about our company?'

✔ You'll gain the foundation to absorb new facts during the interview.

✔ Your preparedness will show you're a headliner, not a bit player.

Figuratively speaking, I hope you won't tie your hands behind your back and put a blindfold around your eyes by failing to gather the data that can change your life. In this chapter, I give you some tips on researching your way to an advantage.

Using Social Media for Background Research

Social media sites like LinkedIn and Facebook are not only great ways to network, find out about upcoming employment opportunities and perhaps even be headhunted, but are also forums where you can find out more about the company you're about to interview for.

Here's how to get started:

✔ If the company you're interviewing for has a Facebook page, follow the page to get up to speed with the organisation's news and events, any new products or services in the works or new directions being taken. If the company doesn't have a Facebook page, find companies in the same sector that do have a page, to get an idea of what's happening in the industry.

✔ Follow the company you're interviewing for on Twitter, or follow similar companies in the industry as well as recruitment agencies that specialise in the sector. This will provide insights into the latest stories, ideas, opinions and news relevant to your job interview.

Expert Aussie career coach Kate Southam says you shouldn't ask people for their views on the company you're about to interview for on a public forum such as Facebook for two reasons. Firstly, you can't control the comments people post in response to your request for info. If the comments are negative about the company, your name will be associated with them and your chances of landing the job might be squashed. Secondly, such a public shout out on social media casts a shadow over your common sense and good judgement — or lack thereof. If you know people who work for the company you're scheduled to interview with — or who have worked there — make discreet inquiries, but even then be prepared to test any information you hear.

Mastering Online Searches

Building a library of free and useful information on most public — and some private — companies is as fast and easy as following directions to 'click here'.

In just an hour or two, you can feast your eyes on these resources:

- ✔ A company's values and mission statement
- ✔ Annual reports
- ✔ Competitor information
- ✔ Financial data
- ✔ General website content
- ✔ Industry trends
- ✔ Information about products and services
- ✔ News releases

You may also be able to find out about

- ✔ Corporate culture
- ✔ Employee views on a company
- ✔ Pending layoffs
- ✔ Pending mergers and acquisitions
- ✔ Shifts in management personnel
- ✔ Stock analysts' views about the company

Consider passing on a job opportunity if you discover a company teetering on a legal edge or planning rounds of redundancies despite promises to deliver stability. But when you discover no impending corporate collapse or toxic bosses running the show, and you want the job, research is still crucial to your performance in the interview.

Asking Questions about Potential Employers

Use the following questions as a checklist to gather all the information you need. (Additionally, see Chapter 10.) You may not be able to find or use information on all the factors that follow, and you may think of others that are not here as important inclusions for your specific sector.

Here's the rule on how much research to do: The more responsible the job — or the more competitive the race — the greater amount of research you must do to pull ahead.

Size and growth patterns

The size of a company and the scope of its operations say a great deal about the company's ambitions and opportunities for advancement. Try to answer the following questions:

- ✔ What industry is the company in?
- ✔ Is the company a market leader or challenger?
- ✔ What are the company's full range of products and services?
- ✔ What is the company best known for?
- ✔ How long has the company's CEO been in place?
- ✔ What is the company's reputation on diversity when hiring and promoting staff?
- ✔ Is the company known for promoting from within?
- ✔ Is the company expanding or downsizing?
- ✔ What are its divisions and subsidiaries?
- ✔ How many employees does it have?
- ✔ Who are its clients and how many does it serve?
- ✔ How many locations does it operate from?
- ✔ Does it have operations overseas?

Direction and planning

Answers to questions about the company's plans can be found through visiting the company's website, viewing its annual report, reading news articles and features in trade publications and websites as well as the business media and by talking to any contacts you have in the relevant industry sector.

The following information is worth pursuing, because it allows you to know some of the hot issues to address or avoid:

- ✔ What are the company's current priorities?
- ✔ What is its mission?

✔ What long-term contracts has it established?

✔ What are its prospects?

✔ What are its problems?

✔ Is it initiating any new products or projects?

Products or services

You don't want to go into a job interview without at least knowing what products or services are the bedrock of the company's business. Find answers to these questions about any company you pursue:

✔ What services or products does the company provide?

✔ What are its areas of expertise?

✔ How does it innovate in the industry — by maintaining cutting-edge products, cutting costs, or what?

Competitive profile and financials

How the company is positioned within its industry and how hard competitors are nipping at its heels are measures of the company's long-term health and the relative stability of your prospective job there. Get to the bottom of these issues by asking some questions:

✔ Who are the company's competitors?

✔ What are the company's current projects?

✔ What setbacks has it experienced?

✔ What are its greatest accomplishments?

✔ Is the company in a growing industry?

✔ Will technology dim its future?

✔ Does it operate with updated technology?

✔ Does it move jobs to another country to access cheaper labour?

Collecting current and accurate information about financials is a long chase, but it's better to learn a company's shaky financial picture before you're hired rather than after you're laid off. Dig for the following nuggets:

- What are the company's sales?
- What are its earnings?
- What are its assets?
- How stable is its financial base?
- Is its profit trend up or down?
- How much of its earnings go to pay employees?
- Is it privately or publicly owned?
- Is it a subsidiary or a division of a big company?
- How deep in debt is the company?
- What external factors are affecting the company's fortunes — such as the cost of materials or the value of the Australian or New Zealand dollar?

Culture and reputation

How fast is the pace? Frantic? Laid-back? Formal? Informal? Aggressive? Answers to the following questions give you clues about a company's culture:

- Does the company run lean on staffing?
- What's the picture on mergers and acquisitions?
- What's its reputation?
- What types of employees does it hire?
- What's the buzz on its managers?
- How does it treat employees?
- Does it push out older workers?

The job role and you

After finding out all the information you can about the company you're interviewing for, take a step back and have a think about how you fit in with the company and the job role.

View recruitment videos with eyes wide open

Companies are rushing to add videos featuring happy employees to their repertoires of recruiting tools. They often present these recruiting videos as a kind of day-in-the-life of a typical employee at ABC Company. They can be very helpful when you watch for clues reflecting the people the company prefers to hire.

The videos are supposed to offer potential employees a glimpse of a company's work environment and culture. For example, a video may show employees seated in a crowded open plan area or exchanging ideas in a futuristic meeting area. If you're an open-space type of person, you'll want to ask about the workspace assignment policy during your interview.

Workforce diversity is another inference you can draw from recruitment videos. What is the age range and gender mix of those in the video?

The videos offer an important tip on how to dress for your interview and the kind of work wardrobe you'd need

in the related job. When everyone in the video is dressed in casual attire and your grooming hallmark is a business suit — or vice versa — you may be at the wrong party.

In an abundance of caution, you may want to watch a company's recruiting video twice. And when you see one that reminds you of an infomercial, put on your critical-thinking cap.

Remember that a company will only show the most positive aspects of working with the team. Happy talkers are chosen to appear on the company's silver screen. Any working environment has good points and bad points but the video will only show the one side. Most videos are only a couple of minutes long so you will probably mainly see employees talking about their jobs rather than doing their jobs at their workstations. This could be just a practical matter or it may be to hide the work environment, so you may need to do more research to get an accurate picture.

Consider the following:

- ✔ How are you going to fit into a company of this size? Perhaps you have experience working for a company of similar size, meaning you can offer insights into growth opportunities and perhaps overseas expansion.

- ✔ Can you recognise any ongoing issues with the company's planning, that you may be able to offer some possible solutions for?

✔ Do you have extensive experience with the products or services this company provides?

✔ Do you have knowledge of the company's competitors? (Without violating confidentiality requirements, of course.)

✔ From what you've been able to work out about the company's culture (frantic or laid-back, for example), how does this fit in with the way you work?

The aim is to be able to use all your research to clarify for the interviewer what you can give to the company, how well you'll fit in and, ultimately, why you're the best candidate.

Extra! Extra! News media resources to the rescue!

When you need to pull out all the stops in preparing for a job you really, really want, turn to media resources for help. You can use a public library to study back-issue indexes and digital archives from the relevant trade media, major newspapers and business magazines and view what has been reported about a particular company or industry sector. Back issues and digital files from *The Age, The Sydney Morning Herald, The Australian Financial Review,* *The New Zealand Herald, Business Review Weekly* in Australia and *The National Business Review* in New Zealand, as well as industry-specific trade journals and newsletters could prove useful. Performing a web search on a company using Google or Bing and then going to the 'news' tab could also turn up interesting nuggets of information. And LinkedIn is a good place to view details about the company executives you will interview with.

Preparation Rocks!

As you approach important job interviews, your research is the first step toward changing your life for the better.

That's because employers consider company research a reflection of your interest and enthusiasm, intelligence and commitment. Research shows that you're thorough, competent and revved up to work. Every employer likes these profit-building or cost-saving traits.

And not so incidentally, finding out what you need to know about a company may encourage you to look elsewhere.

Chapter 6

Understanding Personality Tests

- -

In This Chapter

▶ Understanding why personality tests matter

▶ Uncovering surprising facts about personality tests

▶ Doing your best with proven test tips and sample questions

▶ Learning from the experience and moving on

- -

*T*he online world offers all kinds of unscientific ways for you to plumb your depths — from your taste in music to your choice in colours. But flip that coin to the employment world and personality testing becomes a serious assessment tool that helps decide who gets hired and who gets promoted.

This chapter is a serious close-up on genuine, non-fake, real deal assessments that have become rites of passage in today's workplace.

Wendell Williams, PhD, Managing Director of ScientificSelection. com, is one of the world's leading employment-assessment authorities. Dr Williams is my guide through the psychometric minefield of employment testing.

Personality Testing Means Business

In a nutshell, employers are trying to anticipate why you do what you do at work. That's the reason you may be required to take a *personality test* before being granted an interview or offered a job.

An *integrity test* may or may not be part of the personality assessment. Here's what each measures:

- ✔ Employment personality tests measure choice, preference, values, behaviour, decisions, attitudes and job-related interests.
- ✔ Integrity tests rate honesty, responsibility and reliability.

Test development expert Dr Williams throws more light on the overall reason personality tests have become a favoured business-assessment tool:

> *Employers administer personality and integrity tests because they try to avoid making a bad hire, which means they want to know as much about a potential employee as possible.*

How many companies require job candidates to take personality tests? Estimates are all over the place, topping out at 40 per cent at the time of writing. And a recent survey of Australian human resource managers showed that 69 per cent believed that personality tests are valuable tools that can be used to improve performance. Despite sketchy data, the personality-discovery star is rising. Don't be surprised if you face an online employment personality test in your not-too-distant future.

What You May Not Know about Personality Tests

To borrow from an anonymous saying, 'If you can stay calm while all around you is chaos in the pressure of a pre-employment personality test, then you probably haven't completely understood the seriousness of the situation.' Personality tests, love 'em or loathe 'em, guard the gateways to your future.

The following sections provide a rundown of five important things to understand about your future encounters with personality tests.

Asking questions before the test

Although you can't blow off a request to sit for an employment test and get hired, you can ask a few questions to spread a small safety net under your candidacy. You need to be diplomatic when posing these questions, and confirming your willingness to take part as you ask the questions is a good idea.

Try these feelers:

- ✔ Can I get any feedback regarding test results? How about areas I didn't do well in? At least I'll know what areas need improvement.

- ✔ Will I still be considered for the job if I don't do well on the test?

- ✔ Can you tell me the name of the test I'll be taking, so I can read up on it? I'm curious about what test you use and what has been written about it.

- ✔ Can you tell me how useful the test has been for your company in predicting job performance?

Expect to hear 'no' more often than 'yes' to the preceding questions. If the interviewer is dismissive, it may be just because no-one has ever asked such questions or it could be a sign of what is to come if you land the job. If you think the use of such tests is tough now, wait until you're hired and the honeymoon is over.

Removing the mystique of personality tests

In Australia and New Zealand, personality tests are often referred to as *psychometric* tests. Here's expert Aussie career coach Kate Southam's take on them. These tests are designed to uncover your preferences for different work styles, to see if you're a match for the culture of the organisation. Separate tests may also be used to assess your literacy, numeracy or technical skills.

You can't study for a psychometric test, but you can find sample tests online, and by taking a few of these you can remove the mystery and any nerves you may have about taking such a test. For example, the job board CareerOne.com.au has sample personality and aptitude tests you can take. Go to the CareerOne home page and, under the Career Advice tab, click on Job interviews. You can then look for the links to the sample tests.

When you're completing a test, expect to see a particular type of question repeated throughout the test but using a different wording. The same question being asked in a different way is designed to assess whether your answers are truthful and consistent. Don't get impatient but do look out for these 'repeated' questions. (See the section 'Making the Grade on Job Tests', later in this chapter, for more.)

The jury is still out on just how effective psychometric tests are in predicting job performance or a perfect hire, and an online search will quickly show you how hot the debate runs. Articles in many well-known business and recruitment publications and websites based in the UK, the US and the Australian and New Zealand region continue to attack and defend the use of tests.

However, the important thing for candidates to keep in mind is that if a test is proffered by an employer or recruiter you're dealing with, the last thing that person wants to hear is your opinion about what a time waster such tests are.

To prove valuable, psychometric tests must be *statistically validated*. *Valid* means the test works. Validation studies involve giving the test to hundreds of people and statistically comparing their scores to job performance. You need testing on enough people over enough time to give users confidence that the tests actually predict what the test-makers claim — that they work as advertised.

'Once a company knows what it wants to measure and has chosen a legitimate hiring test, the company studies its own employees to prove test scores are associated with job performance, turnover, training, or other essentials of a successful organisation before judging the test to be validated,' Dr Williams explains.

That's why psychometrically trained professionals are assigned to identify the kinds of psychological traits that lead to the selection of an achieving, profitable workforce. Statistically supportable personality tests typically are written by experienced professionals who take courses in statistics and test design, and hold doctorates in some aspect of applied psychology.

Personality test scores are self-reports. They represent how someone wants to be seen by the world. Scores on personality tests have almost no relationship to actual skills. Don't take the results of a test to heart — move on and embrace the next opportunity. Not all companies use testing to evaluate candidates — or your answers could be just what the next company wants to hear.

Most popular general traits

Widely quoted industrial psychologist Dr Williams reports that university research shows only about five traits are associated with job performance. Although the traits may go by different names, say hello to the Big Five:

- ✔ Conscientiousness about the job
- ✔ Agreeability and flexibility
- ✔ Extroverted behaviour
- ✔ Inquiring mind
- ✔ Non-neurotic

Of the Big Five personality traits, Dr Williams says the three traits most commonly associated with good job performance are conscientiousness, agreeability, and not being neurotic.

Expressed another way, good workers care about their work, get along with others and are emotionally stable.

Who's most likely to use tests

Non-manufacturing businesses tend to use personality tests more than manufacturing industries. Examples of non-manufacturing businesses include retailers, banks, utilities, insurance companies, staffing agencies and communications corporations. High-level executives in any industry generally aren't asked to undergo personality tests. And government departments and agencies typically use their own tests and assessments.

Integrity tests are used in jobs involving money, public safety or merchandise — especially in entry-level positions.

Peeking into privacy issues

'Personality tests need to be handled like confidential medical records,' observes Anne Hart, senior author of *Employment Personality Tests Decoded* (Career Press).

Hart advises candidates to find out how test results are used and what departments, or even outside agencies, the results are shared with.

'Psychological testing, like medical exams, should not be stored in open-ended databases in your employer's human resources department,' Hart adds.

What if you're not hired — how long will your records be kept at the employer's office and/or at the vendor testing company? Under privacy legislation in Australia and New Zealand, you're entitled to know how information about you will be stored, who will see it, what it will be used for and how the information will be disposed of when no longer of use. You can visit the websites of the New Zealand Privacy Commissioner (www.privacy.org.nz) or the Office of the Australian Information Commissioner (www.oaic.gov.au) for more information.

Testing companies in Australia and New Zealand should be willing to discuss their records and security procedures with candidates.

You certainly don't want your test results whizzing around the internet. Underscoring the serious need to protect test score privacy, reports of irreparable damage to someone's reputation do surface. The reports are caused by accidental or malicious posting of another person's personal information online. Even if your records are online for just minutes, they can be copied and distributed around the world for employers to read. You can never be 100 per cent certain that an online image has been killed off. Be sure to ask how test results are stored and protected.

Making the Grade on Job Tests

Conventional wisdom advises that you get a good night's sleep, be truthful in all your answers, and relax and even try to enjoy a personality test that the interviewer says is standard operating procedure.

About the kicked-back mindset, at least, conventional wisdom is wrong. Instead, consider the flower vendor who sells her basket of posies by arranging the freshest pieces on the top. If you want cash for your flowers, learn how to display your best blooms.

In the following sections, I give you tips for displaying your best blooms (traits) in a personality test, tips that I gathered from the four corners of the testing industry.

Visualise yourself fitting in

Based on your research of the company, imagine the ideal candidate. How would that paragon of virtue think? When you hit a wall with a weird question, your fallback position is to try to answer as the ideal candidate or perfect employee.

Obviously, answering as the ideal candidate or perfect employee isn't easy. You need to guess what the paragon is like. (*Hint:* Review video clips featuring employees on the company website.) How much and what kind of personality characteristics are you being compared to?

When in doubt, position yourself as a person of moderation in the mainstream of contemporary thought. Test administrators tend to grade unconventional beliefs as potential trouble.

Company managers prefer to hire people like themselves. Although similarly minded employees don't always do better, a personality kinship gives managers a warm, fuzzy feeling by knowing that everyone looks and talks alike — at least in spirit.

Watch for combination tests

Many tests are combinations of several types of test questions. Even if the first ten questions ask about your personality traits, stay alert for questions about your aptitudes (such as potential for leadership or creativity) or abilities, or your integrity (such as lying). These questions may require greater concentration to answer in ways that will help you.

Beware of absolutes

Watch out for absolutes like *always*, *ever*, and *never*. For example, saying you never took more than your share of things in your life (as in, not even that last piece of chocolate) may paint you as a goody-two-shoes who can't be trusted. For most questions, answer in the middle of the range. But answer integrity questions with full agreement that honesty is the best policy.

Choose answers suggesting positive traits

Try to select answers that put you in the most positive light. Examples of favoured characteristics include

- ✓ Achievement oriented
- ✓ Agreeable
- ✓ Assertive
- ✓ Conscientious
- ✓ Dependable
- ✓ Emotionally stable
- ✓ Good communicator
- ✓ Imaginative
- ✓ Intellectually curious
- ✓ Open to new experiences
- ✓ Optimistic
- ✓ Responsible
- ✓ Sociable
- ✓ Tolerant
- ✓ Trustworthy

Avoid answers suggesting negative traits

Stay away from answers that show you in a less-than-stellar light. Examples of negative characteristics to avoid implying include

- ✔ Acceptance of fraud, as in filing a fraudulent worker's compensation claim
- ✔ Dishonesty
- ✔ Disregard for rules
- ✔ Emotional dysfunction
- ✔ Illegal drug use
- ✔ Inability to function under stressful conditions
- ✔ Lack of self-worth
- ✔ No opposition to stirring up legal trouble
- ✔ Poor impulse control
- ✔ Predisposition for negative interpersonal relationships
- ✔ Prejudice
- ✔ Propensity for interpersonal conflicts
- ✔ Rigidity
- ✔ Tendency to be tense or suspicious
- ✔ Tendency toward time theft (sick leave abuse, tardiness)
- ✔ Thievery

Be alert to replayed questions

As mentioned earlier in this chapter (refer to the section 'Removing the mystique of personality tests'), some tests ask virtually the same question on page one, page three and page ten. The test is trying to catch inconsistencies — figuring you forgot a lie you told 30 questions ago. If possible, read through the test before you start. Consistency counts.

Anticipate integrity test questions

Integrity questioning may be part of a personality test or a separate test.

Special tips for salespeople

The sales representative who maintains long-term relationships selling ongoing telecom services to a company has a different kind of job than does a sales representative who sells an automobile to a customer in a one-time transaction. Personality tests for salespeople differ as well. Even so, any test administered for the sales industry probably measures such core characteristics as the following:

✔ Achievement orientation — a drive for learning new skills and impatiently accomplishing goals

✔ Empathy — the capacity to identify or sympathise with another individual's feelings

✔ High energy — the force to stay with a challenge until you meet it

✔ Intellect — qualities showing culture and imagination

✔ Positive resilience — the ability to not take sales failure personally, and to bounce back for the next sales call

✔ Self-control — a feeling of being in personal control of your destiny

✔ Self-efficacy — the belief that you can meet your expectations if you try hard enough

✔ Self-monitoring — the tendency to use social cues (not only your personal convictions) about what is expected

A lie scale measures the position of a test answer on a gamut from lie to truth. The scale functions as a kind of lie detector by looking for unexpected answers or unusual response patterns.

But even if you're completely fair dinkum, people under pressure of testing sometimes give questionable answers. For example, if you're asked to estimate the percentage of workers who steal from their employers, make a low guess. A high guess may be interpreted to mean you think employee theft is common and, therefore, acceptable.

Most integrity questions are fashioned for entry-level or mid-level workers who have access to merchandise or trade secrets, or for financial workers who handle money.

Take practice personality tests

Ready yourself for employment personality tests by working through a few practice questions and tests. Review free practice tests you find via the web. You will find these tests by typing the most relevant keywords into a browser search engine, such as **sample psychometric tests** or **employment personality tests**.

Free online tests are for educational purposes only and are not intended to be the real deal. Genuine employment personality tests and their answer keys are kept under lock and key. If you're happy to fork out some cash, you can buy access to real deal tests but do your homework first to make sure the test you purchase is relevant to your industry sector.

Can you game the tests?

Many retailers require that applicants score well on a personality test before investing time and money interviewing them, which is why a number of aspirants try to beat the system by bagging the right answers before testing.

A detailed 2009 article in *The Wall Street Journal* created a hornet's nest of reaction in the recruiting industry. It suggested that efforts to screen out unqualified or poor job-fit candidates during these difficult times have created such a competitive environment that job seekers have turned to cheating on work attitude and personality tests (browse online for 'Test for Dwindling Retail Jobs Spawns a Culture of Cheating').

How does the cheating happen? The *WSJ* storyline reported that some job seekers attempt to acquire test-taking savvy by applying to several retailers known to use the same test. Others use surrogate test takers. Still others seek out online answer keys (browse for 'Answers to the Unicru personality test').

Reactions to the idea of gaming the tests are a case of where you stand depending upon where you sit. Test producers insist that gaming can't be done, that it's dishonest and that it's a mistake leading to a job you won't like. But apparently their rationale isn't stopping desperate job seekers from trying anything to gain an interview.

Sample Personality Questions

Questions on all types of tests may require uncomfortable yes/no answers. (Following the questions, I interpret their meaning in parentheses.) Here are some examples:

- *Do you believe that children or spouses are far more important than anything?*

  (Will your family life interfere with your job?)

- *Do you exercise regularly?*

  (Are you likely to be a high risk for sick leave?)

- *I would like to be a florist.*

  (Are your interests suited to this field?)

- *I still maintain close contact with friends from high school.*

  (Do you get along with people for long periods of time?)

- *I have thought of trying to get even with someone who hurt me.*

  (Are you vindictive, or can you put hurts behind you?)

Some questions require specific answers rather than *yes* or *no*:

- *How often do you make your bed?*

  (Do you clean up after yourself? Are you obsessive about it?)

- *On average, how often during the week do you go to parties?*

  (Will you frequently come to work hung over?)

- *Describe how you see work.*

  (Do you see work as mandatory or as a way to obtain rewards?)

Concerned That You Didn't Do Well?

The stark truth is that you can't really do much about a test score when you mess up. Busy employers are focused on finding the right people to hire, not on helping those who are among the unchosen.

'Do-overs are rare,' explains Dr Williams. 'Regardless of what you say or do, most hiring managers have a diehard perception of their favourite personality profiles. If you don't fit their moulds, you seldom get a second chance. In the final analysis, testing is a roll of the dice for the unwary and quicksand for the uneducated.'

Keep On Keeping On

When you've taken a personality test but you weren't invited to an interview, soldier on to your next opportunity. The way to win employment is to keep applying for more jobs.

And remember the words of our old friend Anonymous: 'If at first you do succeed, try to hide your astonishment.'

Chapter 7

Showing You the Money

. . . .

. . . .

*I*magine this uncomfortable scenario: After accepting and starting a new job, you discover that you're paid 20 per cent under market and that, instead of climbing what an enthusiastic recruiter called a stairway to the stars, you're on a road to nowhere.

Fiascos like this can happen when you fall hook, line and sinker for a recruitment pitch that deflects a position's cheapo cash compensation. The pitch distracts you by spotlighting nonmonetary aspects of the position — growth opportunity, the latest technology, fabulous co-workers, super company — you name it.

In this chapter, I list the types of recruiters you're likely to encounter, the siren songs they may sing to snag the best bargains, and the ways you can get the best employment deal for yourself.

First Things First

Although this chapter can help you deal with undermarket offers in general, in a few justifiable exceptions you will and should seriously consider making cash secondary to opportunity or lifestyle in a job you accept. A few examples:

- ✔ You're a new graduate or career changer with scant experience, and you need good breaks and helping hands in a nourishing environment.

- ✔ You're taking a lower rung on a ladder that positions you to compete for a higher rung.

- ✔ You need to spend time elsewhere such as with your children, caring for a parent or family member or on a sport, hobby or part-time business you're serious about.

Special concerns aside, most of the time you're going to zero in on the legal tender you want to earn for the rent of your brains and labour, to maximise cold cash and monetary-based employee benefits. Your first step in your pursuit for fair compensation is finding out salary ranges for the kind of job you're applying for or for someone with your level of experience. The next step is usually negotiations with recruiters.

Recruiters are employers' personal shoppers, tasked with going into the marketplace and bringing back the best-qualified candidates, usually for the best price. Some employers pride themselves on paying above market to attract the best talent or use a salary range to give the organisation wiggle room when negotiating with a new hire.

Finding Out How the Salary Market Works

Knowing your market value — the going rate for people in your industry with skills and a job description similar to yours — is the centrepiece for negotiating the compensation you deserve.

Discovering the market rate for the kind of work you do has never been easier than it is today. Among popular websites offering free salary survey information to job seekers are My Career (mycareer.com.au — click on the Salary tab) and Payscale (www.payscale.com).

My Career provides not only average Australian salary information but also salary information by sector and location, and the best paying sectors. In New Zealand Trade Me provides a comprehensive salary guide by category — go to www.trademe.co.nz/jobs/salary-guide.

Another very useful free resource is the job search engine Indeed.com (www.indeed.com), which reports actual salary ranges currently posted on job boards.

Keep in mind that generalised averages produced by online salary calculators aren't always spot-on for specific companies and jobs.

If you're a member of a professional or industry association, you can ask to see any salary research carried out on your sector. Recruitment firms also publish their own salary surveys, which are based on quizzing candidates and employers. Some examples include Michael Page, Hays, Robert Walters and specialist firms such as Robert Half for accounting and finance, Taylor Root for legal salaries and Greythorn for IT.

Be certain to benchmark the job you're applying for by *job content* — not just by job title. The same job title can mean different things to different people in different companies.

Once you've discovered the market rate for the kind of work you do, you also need to factor in your specific skills and experience. Work out whether what you're bringing to the job means you can expect a little more (or a little less) than market rates.

Background on the bucks

WorldatWork(www.worldatwork.org), an international association of human resource practitioners, is a recognised authority on compensation matters. Here's a selected glossary of WorldatWork terminology:

Cash Compensation

Pay provided by an employer to an employee for services rendered (time, effort and skill). Compensation comprises four core elements:

✔ **Fixed pay:** Also known as *base pay*, fixed pay is nondiscretionary compensation that doesn't vary according to performance or results achieved.

✔ **Variable pay:** Also known as *pay at risk*, variable pay changes directly with the level of performance or results achieved. It's a one-time payment that must be re-established and re-earned each performance period.

✔ **Short-term incentive pay:** A form of variable pay, short-term incentive pay is designed to focus and reward performance over a period of one year or less.

✔ **Long-term incentive pay:** A form of variable pay, long-term incentive pay is designed to focus and reward performance over a period longer than one year. Typical forms include stock options, restricted stock, performance shares, performance units and cash.

Benefits

Programs an employer uses to supplement the cash compensation that employees receive. Some are legally mandated, such as leave entitlements, superannuation or KiwiSaver obligations, and workers' compensation. Others are awarded at the discretion of the employer, such as study assistance, automobiles, and professional group and club memberships.

Discussing Salary and Benefits with Recruitment Consultants

Recruiters are sales professionals, not your new best friends. This is true in all cases — for example, when

✔ The recruiter (also known as a *headhunter*) is an external recruiter (a third-party recruiter or independent recruiter).

✔ An external recruiter is employed as a retained recruiter on an ongoing basis and is paid a set fee — much like a retained lawyer or accountant.

✔ An external recruiter is employed on a transaction basis as a contingency recruiter and is paid only when a submitted candidate is hired.

✔ The recruiter is an internal recruiter (that is, a company recruiter), who is staffed in a company's human resources department and paid a salary.

All recruiters are engaged by employers to find people for jobs — not jobs for people. And they do it by being superb sales professionals.

Recruiters who deem you qualified for a position pass you up to a hiring decision-maker, often the individual to whom you would report.

How can you tell when you're being recruited with a song-and-dance to divert your attention from a chintzy salary? Look out for yourself by discovering the insider secrets in the following sections.

One salary for recruiters, another for employers

Generally, when you're working with a recruiter, you're working with a messenger. They can relay to you the salary range and benefits of the job, and pass on your expectations to the person responsible for making the hiring decision.

Many recruiters advise their client — the employer — on the salary rate for the role. Coming up with a realistic figure, rather than the lowest figure, is in the best interest of the recruiter for two reasons. The first is that they're often paid a percentage of the salary for the role so by driving down the salary, they drive down their cut. Secondly, the recruiter wants to fill the role and a woefully under-market-value salary won't attract a good candidate.

However, in most cases the recruiter doesn't have the ability to make the final decision on your compensation package. Any negotiations that occur between you and a recruiter will need to be confirmed by the person actually doing the hiring.

In the early stages of recruitment, if you make demands for a salary outside the general range for the job being discussed, the recruiter will be the one who has to justify to the person making the hiring decision why you're worth more.

The best approach is to keep your salary discussions with the recruiter general, and discuss specifics directly with the hiring manager. (See the section 'Stalling Money Talk with Smart Replies' for more on delaying salary discussions.)

Handling salary boxes in online applications

Recently I was asked for a practical way to handle the *salary requirement* and *salary history* (two different things) questions when either or both are embedded as required fields in an online application. B.I. (before internet), you could write 'Negotiable' for salary expectation, to keep from under- or overpricing yourself. But most online applications won't accept 'Negotiable' (or 'Open' or 'Will discuss in an interview') for expected salary as a viable answer, so that tactic is out history's window. What now?

Jack Chapman (www.salarynegotiations.com) rides to the rescue. Salary consultant and workshop leader, Chapman is the author of the best-selling guide *Negotiating Your Salary: How to Make $1,000 a Minute* (Mount Vernon Press, 2011), my favourite book in the genre. Here's what Chapman told me about working those windows:

> *Your self-interest is best served by putting whatever number in the salary-requirement box that you think won't get you screened out. The employer is essentially asking, 'Can we afford you?' Since you won't require anything other than a competitive salary, your answer, by putting in a competitive number, is 'Yes, you can afford me.'*

> *This strategy works nicely when the box is titled 'Salary Requirements' or 'Expected Salary', but requires an additional step if it is labelled 'Current Salary'. Once you're in the interview, you'll need to explain that you interpreted 'Current Salary' to mean 'Current Salary Requirements', and if they want a 'Salary History', you'll be glad to provide it later as needed.*

Who wins, who loses on a lowball offer

When you're working with a contingency recruiter who encourages you to take less than the going rate for a job, the recruiter may have your best interests at heart. Or the recruiter may just want to close the job order quickly.

A contingency recruiter's fee is based on your first-year earnings. Follow this admittedly oversimplified example: Say the recruiter is to be paid 15 per cent of the job's first-year salary. If the job's market rate is $100,000, the recruiter would earn a $15,000 fee. But when the job's budget figure is under market — say, only $90,000 — the recruiter takes a hit of $1,500, compared to your loss of $10,000.

From the contingency recruiter's viewpoint, most of a loaf is better than none. And the recruiter hopes for future assignments from the employer that can more than compensate for losing relatively few dollars on a single transaction.

Negotiating in the Moment

After all your salary prep, the time has arrived to reap your rewards: You're in the interview room, and the back-and-forth begins.

But just when the interview is starting to fly, *bam!* — the interviewer lets go with a dangerous question that can severely clip your wings: *How much money are you looking for?* Should you name your price right then and there? Not if you can help it.

A salary request that's too low devalues your abilities; a salary request that's too high looks like you're too big for the company budget. Both bids leave you out of luck. Be aware that some employers have already budgeted for the position, and the first offer is their best offer. They ask what you want merely to confirm that the money's enough to interest you in the job.

Instead of specifying your salary too early, use the tips in the following sections to help you first discuss the requirements of the job more fully.

Your compensation should be based on the value of the job someone wants to pay you to do, not on the value of the job someone has paid you to do in the past.

Giving and taking at the right times

Sure, you have a pretty good idea going in about the remuneration you're shooting for, but you may discover wildcards while you're in the interview. You knew, for instance, that the job requires travel, and you figured maybe 25 per cent of your time would be spent on the road, but now the interviewer reveals the true travel requirement — 75 per cent. Would that revelation cause you to rethink the money or re-evaluate whether you should accept the job at any salary?

Moreover, if you have to talk salary too early in the interviewing process, a decision-maker may not yet be sufficiently smitten with you to make the company's best offer.

What is the single best thing you can do to receive a higher pay offer when you're interviewing for a job? Delay discussing salary until you're offered (or nearly offered) a specific position.

Until you have the offer, the employer holds all the weight. Once you have the offer, the scales shift. You have something the employer wants, and you become equals negotiating a business proposition. From outsider, you have become poised to become the newest insider — a good place to be.

Learning to deflect salary questions until the timing shifts to your advantage can greatly influence the amount of money that you take from the bargaining table.

Although the advice to sit tight until the timing is right is still on the mark, doing so is easier said than done in the current market, says salary negotiation pro Jack Chapman. He explains:

> In the 1980s, it was easy to postpone the salary talk. That has changed over the years. Employers are more demanding or inquisitive or something. Yet the principle is the same — postpone when and if you can without appearing difficult.

When you're pressured to talk money sooner rather than later, Chapman warns that digging in your heels and flat-out refusing to comply is a mistake. By being hard-nosed, you set up a power struggle that you can't win. You'll be seen as obstinate and hard to work with. A power struggle can cost you the job.

Sometimes you can just ask

To make certain your salary research is on target, network in professional groups. At association meetings, speak to people in a position to hire you. Work the conversation around to asking a question: 'What can someone with my skill set expect to earn in your organisation?'

Nor should you move to the other extreme, in which you meekly cave in, tell all and let it go at that. Just as a dogmatic refusal earns you a label of being too strong, a roll-over-and-scratch-my-belly response may make you seem too weak.

Moreover, when you're too low or too high for the company's budget, you hand the employer's interviewing screener information to judge you by your price, not by your whole package of qualifications. Even in the final interview round, premature dollars talk may lead a decision-maker to see you as too expensive without your being given an opportunity to justify your worth and negotiate.

Fortunately, you have a better way to connect when you're giving away your bargaining leverage too soon: Get a quid pro quo.

What markers do you want as IOUs for your upfront compliance? You want agreement that your early money talk won't screen you out of further interview opportunities. And you want agreement that your salary discussion will focus on the market value of the position and not on your salary history.

To sidestep the negative consequences of early revelation as much as possible, you want fair consideration. What you can say to get fair consideration differs a little depending on the interviewing situation. (Find out about the differences between screening and selection interviews in Chapters 2 and 4.)

Here are Chapman's illustrations of what you can say in three situations:

> ✔ **Phone screening:** *Before I give you all that information, can I ask a question? (Yes.) I don't know who you'll hire, but from what I've seen so far, you should definitely at least interview me. If I'm forthright about all my compensation factors, can I be assured of an interview?*

✔ **Interview screening:** *Before I give you all that information, can I ask a question? (Yes.) I don't know who you'll hire, but from what I've seen so far, I would definitely like to participate in the second round of interviews. If I'm forthright about all my compensation factors, can I be assured of that?*

✔ **Selection interviewing:** *Before I give you all that information, can I ask a question? (Yes.) I'm a little concerned that we could lose a perfectly good match over salary expectations. And I'm confident that you'll pay a competitive salary — which is all I need. Can you first give me your rough range, your ballpark compensation, and I'll be candid and tell you how that compares?*

If you're too high or too low, Chapman's approach gives you the opportunity to address the discrepancy in the interview process instead of having the employer decide behind closed doors with no input from you.

Understanding why salary questions come early

Some interviewers know exactly what they're doing by front-loading the salary question; others may just be feeling their way through the process. The salary question comes up quickly when the interviewer

✔ Is trying to instantly determine your professional level, or is slyly probing to see whether you'll be happy with the low side of an offer.

✔ Wants to test the market. The interviewer may not even have an idea of the position's market value and is shopping candidates to simplify budgeting.

✔ Is open to paying whatever is necessary to get the right person and just wants to know what he's in for.

Whatever the interviewer's motivation for prying a salary disclosure from you, without a job offer, salary disclosures put too much power in the employer's hands. That point was confirmed to me by an HR executive (who, understandably, wishes to remain anonymous): 'While I may request salary histories from others, I never comply with that demand when I'm in the job market. Why not? I know a guillotine when I see one — I design them.'

Tell recruiters your salary history

Should you ever disclose your salary history or salary expectations before a job offer? Yes. Tell all when you're asked by third-party employment specialists — chiefly, executive recruiters and employment consultants who find people for jobs.

These professionals are specialists at their work and are paid for their time, on either a retained or contingency basis. They get paid to find good talent, and so they won't let salary deter them from presenting you when your skills are a match for a job opening. Recruiters are far too busy with the matchmaking task to waste time with you if you make their work difficult. Time is money.

So what should you do when the salary question comes at you too soon? What can you gracefully say to hold off a precipitate discussion? The following section, 'Stalling Money Talk with Smart Replies', gives you a number of script lines to use in response to premature questions about your salary expectations. They're followed by lines useful in sidestepping a salary history so low that interviewers will wonder why — if you're such a standout candidate — you've been so grossly underpaid in the past.

Stalling Money Talk with Smart Replies

Don't let a frog clog your throat when an interviewer presses for the salary discussion before you've established your value. Instead, answer along the following lines:

> *I'm sure that money won't be a problem after I'm able to show you how my qualifications can work to your advantage, because they closely match your requirements.*

> *My salary requirements are open to discussion. Your company has a reputation of being fair with employees, and I trust you would do the same in my case. I don't think salary will be a problem if I'm the right person for the job.*

I'm aware of the general range for my kind of work, but I'd feel better talking about pay once we've established what specific performance goals the job calls for.

I'd be kidding if I said money isn't important to me — sure, it is! But the job itself and the work environment are also very important to me. I wonder if we can hold the pay issue for a bit?

I'm a great believer in matching pay with performance, so I can't speak with any certainty about the kind of money I'm looking for until I know more about what you need.

Money is not my only priority; I'd really like to discuss my contributions to the company first — if that's okay with you.

I can't answer that question until I know more about this job.

The amount of my starting compensation is not as much of an issue to me as how satisfying my filling the position will be for both of us. Can we talk more about what the position entails?

Before we get into the compensation issue, can you tell me more about the kind of skills and the type of individual you're looking for to help you reach your goals? What do you expect the person you hire to accomplish within the first three months?

All I need is fair market value for the job's demands, which I'm sure you'll pay, so is it okay if we talk about the details of the job first?

As far as I can tell, the position seems like a perfect fit for me — tit for tat on your requirements and my qualifications. So as long as you pay in the industry ballpark, I'm sure that we won't have a problem coming up with a figure we're both happy with.

Before we can come to an agreement, I need to know more about your strategy for compensation, as well as confirm my understanding of the results you're looking for. Can we hold that question for a bit?

Since pay includes so many possibilities for compensation, I'd like to first know more about your

*compensation plan overall and how it relates to the
position.*

*I'm sure that you have a fair salary structure, and if I'm the
best candidate for the position we can work something out
that we'll all like.*

*I'm not used to talking money before a job offer; are you
making me an offer?*

*I will consider any reasonable offer. Should we talk about
it after we've wrapped up the details of the job, and I've
been able to show you what I bring to your company?*

*I'm paid roughly the market value of a [occupational
title] with [number of years'] experience and the
ability to [manage, or do something special]. If you're
competitive with the market, there won't be a problem
with salary.*

Considering More Factors That Affect Job Pay

In addition to the timing of the offer, the size of the company
influences how high the interviewer will bid for you. Although
large companies typically pay more, small companies without
formal pay structures are easier to negotiate with than corporate
titans.

But even at huge companies where pay scales are cut and dried,
your potential boss may have the latitude to cut you a better
deal. In fact, some interviewers see your negotiation attempts at
improving your compensation as a desirable trait — yet another
indicator that they've made the right choice. Their reasoning: *If
you can look after your own best interests, you can look after ours.*

Other factors identified by negotiation authority Jack Chapman
that influence the size of pay offers include the following:

- ✔ **Supply and demand:** In employee-driven markets, salary
  offers tend to rise; in employer-driven markets, salary
  offers don't rise and may even fall.
- ✔ **Special skills:** Skills in short supply may merit
  premium pay.

- ✔ **Urgency:** A company losing revenue because a job goes unfilled may offer higher pay.

- ✔ **Recruiting fatigue:** A company weary of failure in filling a position may ease salary limits.

- ✔ **Salary compression:** Concern that paying you a higher wage may lead to revolt by current employees can cause a company to stick rigidly to a certain salary.

Getting Your Worth's Money

Oh, happy day. Your interviewer looks you straight in the eye and says, 'We'd like you to join our team; I'm offering you a job, but before we go any further, we should talk about how much you'd like to be paid.' The moment of truth has arrived. You've got the offer. No more dodging the money issue.

To nab the best offers, follow the guidelines in the sections that follow.

Finding your place in the range

The market rate that big companies typically pay for a job is often stated in a range with a minimum, midpoint and maximum salary. Smaller companies may not operate on such a formal spectrum.

Negotiating doctrine has long insisted that he who goes first in a price negotiation loses. To follow classic counsel, when you're offered (or virtually offered) a job and are asked to name your price, bounce the ball back into the interviewer's court: *Can I ask you to take the lead on this question — can you tell me your range for this position?* (If you did your homework, you already know the range. You're merely asking for confirmation.)

Most often the interviewer who doesn't mind tossing the first figure on the table will respond with a straightforward answer. But anecdotes abound in recruiting circles about interviewers who try to save the company a few dollars by purposely misrepresenting the midpoint to be the maximum salary. For example, suppose you're applying for a job that through research you've learned is budgeted at between $50,000 and $60,000. To your surprise, the interviewer claims that $55,000 is the maximum wage. And you know it's really the midpoint. Hmmm.

Polite probing is one way to respond: *I'm not sure I heard you correctly, or perhaps my research is wrong. Did you say that $55,000 [midpoint figure] is the high end of the range for this position? I thought it was $60,000, which fits in my range.*

But when the interviewer bounces the ball right back into your court and you have to go first or look like a sock puppet, express your salary requirements in a range based on the going rate for the job: *I'd be expecting salary in the range of [$58,000 to $65,000]. I think that's a range we can work with, don't you?*

Citing a range is good because it gives you haggling room and shows that you're economically aware.

Not sure where you realistically should land in the range? Match your request to your experience level. The following guidelines show you how:

- ✔ Don't ask for bottom of the range unless you're a rookie. Even then, if you've worked while in school, ask for a two-striped corporal's pay rather than a one-striped private's. You're positioning yourself as a top rookie candidate.

- ✔ A conservative school of thought recommends that experienced people ask for a pay point just above midrange — to show not only that you're above average, but also that you understand the need to leave room for raises.

- ✔ Highly qualified candidates head toward the top of the company's projected range, where they belong.

Plot your salary history carefully

Bear in mind that salary is a cash figure; total compensation includes benefits and such variable pay as potential annual bonuses, stock options and expected merit raises. Example: *Last year I earned $42,000 to $45,000 compensation, based on a salary of $30,000.* (Review the sidebar titled 'Background on the bucks' earlier in this chapter.)

When your salary history ranks you at the top or above the range of market value, you can afford to discuss that history verbatim.

When your history is less impressive, be less specific. State your figures in wide ranges so that you're more likely to stay in the game for positions for which you're qualified. Include figures slightly above and below the market value to cover all your bases. Usually this approach requires bundling your income figures for multiple years: *For the past three years, I have earned total annual compensation ranging from $95,000 to $125,000 for my work in this field.*

Some job seekers feel they should inflate their salary histories. That's a risky idea — the odds of discovery are stacked in the employer's favour.

Instead of misrepresenting your history to try to improve your lot in salary negotiations, try the following:

✔ Show compensation modules. List base pay and variable pay in one figure; give another figure for benefits; then add the figures together for the total compensation package.

✔ At executive levels, list compensation items line by line.

You may be asked to back up your salary claims. Decide in advance what you will do if your interviewer asks you for tax notices of assessment or pay slips. The request isn't illegal, but you're also perfectly within your rights to refuse. So you should anticipate whether you will comply.

Some job seekers adamantly refuse to supply a salary history and give a middle-finger salute to requests for one. They look at their pay records as a supreme privacy issue and may feel that they're grossly underpaid — which is the reason they're looking for another job. As one job seeker anonymously commented online: 'I don't want to work for a company that demands to know my salary. I want to work for a company that wants me and will do whatever it takes to get me.' I applaud that sentiment but know that a dogged flat refusal is unlikely to produce the most invitations to audition.

When the offer isn't right

When the salary you've been offered isn't as high as you'd expected, or is at the lower end of the established range, you have a few options, covered in this section.

Stonewalled? Try to upgrade the job

When you've established what the position entails and you're told you've received the best offer and that the job isn't worth more, try to make the position more important in the scheme of things. Here are some strategies to boost the importance of the job:

- ✔ Point out that the job requires more than the standard duties suggested by the job title — that the job's content fits into a job description that merits a higher pay bracket. Clarify how you plan to minimise company costs through your performance. Explain how you'll pay for yourself. By using this tactic, you more firmly establish your worth to the company and justify your performance-based reason for asking a higher price.

- ✔ Beef up the job. I once became one of the highest-paid managers in an organisation by combining two positions and creating a new job title. An employer may be interested in considering a 'two-for-one' who is paid a 'one-and-a-half' salary.

Even if you don't succeed in your upgrade move, you'll have put your new boss on notice that you're ready to see the money.

Use dramatic silence

What should you do when the interviewer offers you a salary on a lower level of the salary range for the position? Two words: Keep quiet!

As the interviewer finishes the offer and waits for your reply, let the interviewer wait for enough time to notice your silence. Everyone has trouble outwaiting 30 seconds of silence. Look at the floor. Keep your face glum.

These moments of nonverbal communication show your dissatisfaction with the offer, without a word to incriminate you as overly hungry for money. The interviewer may feel compelled by this uncomfortable silence to improve the offer — or at least open a dialogue in which you can campaign for other kinds of rewards.

Don't try this technique on video interviews; refer to Chapter 3 to find out how to handle these unique interview situations.

Finding web-based negotiation help

Continue learning all you can about the ins and outs of getting employers to show you the money. Here are three suggestions:

✔ Visit Jack Chapman's website, Salary Negotiations (www.salary negotiations.com).

✔ The Australian Businesswomen's Network blog has some excellent information on topics such as business development and social media. For extra help with negotiating the best starting salary, check out www.abn.org.au/blog/negotiating-best-starting-salary.

✔ Online salary calculators noted earlier in this chapter under the headline 'Finding Out How the Salary Market Works' provide a number of responsible how-to articles.

Turn to words of last resort

When it seems as though the right numbers just aren't on your radar, you have little to lose by trying a straightforward response:

> *It pains me to say this. While I'm very attracted to what we've been discussing, the figure you named is just not an incentive for me to join your group. The good news is that we're both interested, so let's keep talking. What do you think?*

No flexibility? Make creative suggestions

In negotiating with a small company, you're less likely to encounter fixed pay policies, permitting you to get creative about your compensation package. If a small company can't afford you on a cash basis, what else do you want?

You have a wide range of options for sweetening an offer. Ask for some combination of the following:

✔ Additional paid annual leave days

✔ A company car

- An early salary review
- An expense account
- Extra-generous kilometre reimbursement
- Parking privileges
- Recreational or day-care facilities
- Stock options
- Tuition reimbursement

If you're negotiating for a job that pays below $30,000 and you know the company's salary cap can't be raised right now, try to get a shorter workweek or flexible work hours, and take a second job to keep a roof over your head. If you already have a car, maybe you can trade the company car for cash.

Chapter 8

Dressing for Success

. . . .

In This Chapter

▶ Mastering the art of interview dressing

▶ Noting the dress code requirements that stay constant

▶ Keeping up with fashion trends in your type of job

▶ Surveying conservative versus business casual

. . . .

*T*he clothes on your back are the tip-off to the line of work you're in. Any observer over the age of five knows that Lady Gaga is an entertainer, not a firefighter or a police officer.

Sports team members wear their own colour-coded costumes, dentists favour white coats and religious clerics don ceremonial clothing. Bankers dress to impress in hand-tailored dress suits, and laboratory technicians dress to survive in chemical coveralls.

When you want to launch your career — or take it up a notch, or pull it back from the edge — you need the right wardrobe for your job interviews. You want your clothes, accessories and grooming to make a smash-hit first impression because first impressions strongly affect the entire interview.

This chapter details how to impress the hiring squad by selecting interviewing attire that boosts your confidence. When you look good, you feel great — and you act better.

You Are What You Wear

'Send a message through your clothing and be aware of the details,' is solid advice from international business dress expert Barbara Pachter, who lectures, consults and writes on the topic.

So what are the wrong messages to send? Pachter (www.
pachter.com) cuts to the chase, naming eight ways your
interview attire could sink your chances:

- **Wearing clothes that are too big:** You'll look like a little kid
  in your big brother or sister's clothing! Your clothing needs
  to fit.

- **Wearing skirts that are too short:** A short skirt draws
  attention to legs. Is that where you want people to look?

- **Showing cleavage:** Sexy isn't a corporate look. Low-cut
  tops that expose cleavage are just not appropriate in the
  office.

- **Wearing short socks:** Socks that are too short can expose
  skin and hairy legs when men sit or cross their legs.

- **Using colour to draw attention to your clothing:** Do you
  want to be remembered for what you said or what you
  wore? A man wearing bright green slacks, which are not
  typical corporate clothing, would probably be labelled as
  'the green-pants man'.

- **Wearing clothing with inappropriate messaging or design:**
  A candidate wearing a shirt with small teddy bears won't
  get the job — his interviewers will just be talking about his
  shirt.

- **Forgetting about your shoes:** People notice shoes. Your
  shoes must be clean, polished and in good condition, and
  appropriate for the employer organisation. No night club
  shoes or sandals, please.

- **Ignoring your grooming:** Your clothes need to be clean
  and pressed. No safety pins for buttons. No holes. No frays.
  No chipped nail polish. No nose hairs. They are job offer
  killers.

Starting Well to End Well

You set the stage for the *halo effect* when you make your
appearance appropriate for the job you seek. That is, when the
interviewer likes you right away, the interviewer may assume
that if you excel in one area (your image), you excel in others.
Some potential employers make a subconscious hiring decision
within seconds of meeting a candidate and spend the rest of the
interview validating their initial impression. With these stakes in
mind, be sure your appearance is a real curtain raiser.

Minding the Three Commandments of Style

By choosing appropriate clothing for the job, you signal to employers that you respect their company's culture and that you care enough to expend the effort to make the right impression.

Begin your mastery of interviewing impressions with these three key principles of dressing yourself in the right team uniform.

Dress to fit the job and the job's culture

Social DNA draws people to others who are like them. When extending a warm welcome to a newcomer, you pay compliments that communicate the message 'You're one of us.'

Companies and organisations are made of people working as a group to accomplish common goals. An anthropologist may think of such a group as a kind of workplace tribe.

When your choice of clothing or your grooming keeps you from looking as though you're a member of the tribe, you create an image of an outsider, perhaps causing the interviewer to perceive you as 'not one of us.' You must make the effort to look as though you absolutely belong in the organisation.

How can you find out about the company's dress code and grooming conventions? You have several options:

- Visit the company's website and search for videos of employees. Pay attention to how employees dress at the level of position you seek — clerk, manager or executive.

- Check for beards, moustaches and long, loose hair. Notice whether the men are wearing casual jackets or suits, or simply shirts with or without a tie. Observe whether the women are in pants or skirts.

- Call the human resources office and ask about the company's dress code.

- ✔ If you have found the job through a recruiter, ask the consultant about dress code before meeting the employer. Such a question will score you extra points with the recruiter too.

- ✔ Use your personal network — or an online social network — to find an employee whom you can quiz.

- ✔ Visit the workplace and observe employees coming and going.

Correctly interpreting the company dress code is the Number One Commandment to follow in dressing for job interviews.

Think of interviewing attire as a costume

As I emphasise repeatedly in this chapter, interview attire is a work-related costume of sorts. With a few exceptions, which I touch on later in this chapter under 'Selecting creative fashion', the job interview is not an outlet for flaming self-expression.

(A rookie job seeker once debated this point with me, insisting on her right to wear whatever she chose to wear to an interview: 'My personal style and how I look is my business,' she petulantly insisted. 'True,' I agreed, 'and the person an interviewer chooses to hire is the interviewer's business.')

When you're not sure whether your interview wardrobe borders on bizarre or is more appropriate for after-hours wear, apply this litmus test: *Would my favourite film director cast me as a person portraying XYZ employee if I auditioned for the part wearing this get-up?*

By wearing an interview-appropriate outfit, you're not selling out your authentic self; you're moving on. And if fortune and preparation smile, you're moving on to a better place: Making the shortlist of candidates and then being hired is the goal when attending a job interview.

'Look the part, and the part plays itself'

The old theatre adage in this section's heading is the Number Three Commandment in constructing your interview image, says Jack D Stewart, a retired recruiter.

Stewart once accepted a recruiting search for an industrial sales rep that came from a new client. Stewart's firm began referring quality candidates, recommending to the candidates that they dress conservatively for their interviews, meaning business suits, well-pressed shirts and silk ties.

Six interviews with different individuals brought the same puzzling response from the new client: 'Each candidate was basically qualified, but not what we're looking for.'

Stewart's firm had a policy of re-evaluating a client's assignment when six candidates were referred and none received a job offer. A recruiter was sent to the client's offices to uncover the problem.

Imagine the recruiter's astonishment when he entered an office filled with people dressed in very casual trousers and shirts sans ties. Well, the recruiter thought, these must be the foot soldiers. What does the captain wear? The recruiter found out soon enough when the sales manager arrived to greet him in a pair of black work shoes topped by white socks.

'From that day forward,' Stewart explains, 'we dressed down our candidates for their interviews with that client — but we couldn't bring ourselves to tell them to wear white socks. Finally, one of our referrals was hired. The experience is a good reminder for job interviewees: *When in Rome, wear a toga.*'

Changing with the Times: Dress Codes

Is the following statement true or false? 'You can never be overdressed. Even if they say to wear business casual, it's appropriate for you to be in a suit and tie.'

If you guessed 'true', you probably guessed wrong.

A new wind is blowing into Australian and New Zealand workplaces defining what constitutes acceptable clothing to wear on the job. And to a certain extent, the lightening up on dress codes has spilled over into job interviewing.

First, a little background: I can't remember a time when virtually every job interviewing expert hasn't hammered home the basic tenet that dressing conservatively is the safest route. End of discussion.

That advice often retains validity, but here's the thing: For many people, the notion of what dressing conservatively means has changed. Traditional suit-and-tie wisdom is no longer universally and automatically correct. *Conservative*, in many cases, now means carefully selected business-casual apparel.

Can you be overdressed?

A handful of studies over the past decade confirm that workplace dress codes have become more liberal than they were back in the starchier 20th-century days:

- A worldwide Reuter's poll of 12,500 workers conducted in 2010 found that 40 per cent of respondents said they wear casual clothes at work.

- Focus groups conducted at the University of Tasmania found that younger people tend to be more individualistic than older generations, and they like to express this individualism via their clothing. So as more of the younger generation enters the workforce, the push for more casual clothing while at work is increasing.

- A 2011 survey on behalf of CareerBuilder (2,500 US hiring managers and 3,900 US workers) found that employers are becoming more relaxed about dress codes. Of these, 15 per cent reported they are right now changing to a more casual dress code.

- A tally of employers conducted by the US National Association of Colleges and Employers revealed that companies seem to be considerably more relaxed about appearance these days. Just 12 per cent said that a male job candidate wearing an earring would be a negative, and only 28 per cent said they'd frown at weird hair colour (like blue, green or violet).

The casual and laid-back dressing trend started working its way across Australia and New Zealand workplaces during the dawn of the tech era in the late 1990s and has moved beyond workers who work alone or in creative groups.

Even public-meeting sales professionals have jumped on the casual fashion runway — but not all. Many, such as those in medical, pharmaceutical and financial investments sales, continue to wear a suit.

What to do about body art

While some companies continue to drop the curtain on job seekers with tattoos and body piercings, the practice is now so common that employers would be severely limiting their candidate pool if they rejected everyone with a tat or a nose ring.

Workplace authority John A Challenger says overall attitudes to body art in particular have softened. CEO of global outplacement firm Challenger, Gray & Christmas, Challenger says, 'With everyone from soccer moms to MIT computer science graduates sporting tattoos, preconceptions about tattooed individuals are no longer valid. More importantly, companies have a vested interest in hiring the most qualified candidates.'

A 2010 Pew Research Centre report on people aged 18 to 29 reveals that 38 per cent have ink. Tattooed Gen Xers aged 30 to 45 came in at a close 32 per cent. In Australia, consumer watchdog Choice estimated in 2013 that a quarter of those aged under 30 sport tattoos. As for bling, nearly one in four people aged 18 to 29 has a piercing somewhere other than the earlobe. (Your guess on its location is as good as mine.)

However, a survey carried out by Brisbane recruiting firm Employment Office in 2012 found 60 per cent of respondents believe visible tattoos are unacceptable in the workplace and an even higher number claim they should be covered up during a job interview.

Should you dress 10 per cent above your level?

When you go job interviewing, the classic advice is, 'Dress one step up from what you'd typically wear to work in that position.' Other lines you may hear are 'Dress 10 per cent better than you ordinarily would' or 'Dress for the position you'd like to have one day, so you'll be seen as promotable.'

My take on upscaling for interview days is to 'Dress the best you're ever going to look in the job you're competing for.'

Whether you cover up or display your body art depends on the sector you're joining as well as the attitude of the person interviewing you. Don't expect to see body art or piercings on display in sectors such as legal, accounting and professional services. On the flip side, in advertising, technology and design, body art may be no big deal.

Use commonsense at all times and if in any doubt, err on the side of caution. When your research of a company's dress code is still thumbs down on tattoos and body piercings, cover up the ink and remove the bling — or pass on the interview. Maybe it's not the place for you.

Selecting from the Basic Types of Interview Wardrobes

Both women and men should expect every nuance of their appearance to be noted and interpreted at a job interview. As Mark Twain supposedly said, 'Clothes make the man. Naked people have little or no influence on society.'

When you're getting ready for the big days, choose your attire from these four basic fashion categories:

- **Conservative:** Examples of conservative dressing environments include banks, law offices, accounting firms and management offices — especially in big corporations.

- **Business casual:** Business-casual environments and career fields include information technology, sales, government agencies, education, retail, real estate, engineering, small companies and internet firms. (*Smart casual* — a term sometimes interchangeably used with *business casual* — means a loosely defined but pulled-together informal look for both men and women.)

✔ **Work casual:** Work casual environments are those that require work clothes suited to the task such as for construction, trucking, maintenance, repair, landscaping and other jobs where work clothes may end the day stained and sweaty.

✔ **Creative fashion:** Clothing worn in career fields such as entertainment, fashion, graphic design, interior design, popular music and other arts can be more creative and 'fashion forward'.

A discussion of each category follows.

Remaining conservative

Conservative dressing means no surprises. Your look is traditional or restrained in style. You avoid showiness. You aren't flamboyant. Conservative dressing means you not only wear the established team uniform, but also wear it well, from the tip of your white collar to the closed toe of your dark shoes.

For *women*, a conservative checklist includes the following:

✔ **Suit:** Wear a two-piece suit or a simple dress with a jacket. Good colours are navy blue, grey, dark green, dark red, burgundy and black. Make sure your skirt length is a bit below the knee or not shorter than just above the knee.

In a dark colour, a pantsuit is a tasteful choice. Accessorise it with a simple scarf or brooch. *Caveat:* If your research shows you're interviewing with a super-traditionalist, stick to skirts.

About that fragrance

Perfumes and after-shave scents should be minimal or missing. A number of people are allergic; others may be reminded by the fragrance of someone they didn't enjoy knowing.

✔ **Shirt:** A white, off-white, or neutral-coloured blouse is a safe choice.

✔ **Shoes:** Closed-toe pumps with low heels or mid-heels (3 to 5 centimetres) suggest that you're work-minded.

✔ **Accessories:** Laptop bags in leather or contemporary briefcases and an understated quality handbag are fine. A watch and simple jewellery are also appropriate but avoid distracting jewellery or watches and anything that jingles.

✔ **Make-up:** Moderate make-up for daytime wear is appropriate.

✔ **Hair:** Simply styled hair looks contemporary; observe styles on TV news presenters and public business figures, for whom maintaining a professional image is essential.

For *men*, the following conservative checklist applies:

✔ **Suit:** Power-suit colours are navy or charcoal grey. (Black on men is seen as sombre.) Tans and medium-tone colours work well if your research shows they're included in the company's colour chart for team uniforms. Suits should be well tailored — nothing too tight or too baggy.

✔ **Shirt:** White is the first choice for shirts; blue is second. In either case, wear only long sleeves.

✔ **Tie:** Dark or low-key (blue, black, navy or grey) or power-red colours bring to mind executives. Geometric patterns are okay, but only if they're minimal. Be sure your necktie knot is neat and centred on your neck; the bottom of the tie should just reach your belt. Skip the bowtie.

✔ **Shoes:** Wear lace-up shoes in the same colour as your belt. Wear black shoes if your suit is grey or navy; wear dark brown shoes for tans or medium-tone colours — in both cases, choose polished and clean shoes that are in good condition. Rubber-soled shoes are a bad match for a professional suit and tie, as are alligator shoes or sandals.

✔ **Socks:** Wear dark socks in mid-calf length so no skin shows when you sit down.

✔ **Accessories:** Limit jewellery to a wristwatch and, if you wear them, cufflinks.

Online wardrobe mistresses and masters

Fashion-focused websites are the perfect media to track the latest fashion scene (what's hot and what's not seems to change every 15 minutes). For starters, try these sites:

✔ *Vogue Australia*'s Spy Style (www. vogue.com.au/blogs/ spy+style): A collective of Australia's best fashion bloggers, as selected by the editors of *Vogue Australia*.

✔ The Iconic (www.theiconic. com.au): A guide to the latest Australian fashion as well as global trends, the site includes a blog covering women's and men's fashion.

✔ Isaac Likes (www.isaaclikes. com): A popular fashion blog by New Zealander Isaac Hindin-Miller covering all aspects of menswear, from photo shoots to fashion shows, as well as his own take on men's style.

Cruising business casual

An increasing number of recruiters say that a business suit is too formal for an interview at their company. (Remember the true story earlier in this chapter with the punch line 'When in Rome, wear a toga'? Refer to the section 'Look the part, and the part plays itself' for more.)

The interpretation of *business casual* varies too widely for universally accepted rules, but mainstream opinion nixes casual clothing you'd wear to a picnic or the footy, such as track pants, exercise wear, shorts, T-shirts with slogans or commercial logos, bare midriffs, halter tops and singlets.

For *women*, a business casual checklist includes the following:

✔ **Clothing:** Guidelines here are looser than for conservative dress. Sticking with the following points is a safe bet:

- A casual jacket or blazer with well-pressed trousers or a skirt is a top option.
- A jacketed tailored dress is a fine choice.
- Tailored knit sweaters and sweater sets are appropriate.

- A skirt that's knee length or longer, paired with a blouse, works well for support jobs.

- Avoid pastel overload (pink, baby blue); those colours may work great for a nursery but not for your professional outfit.

- Provocative clothing (see-through tops, uncovered cleavage, second-skin pants, shimmering fabric, super-short skirts) isn't your best look for offers at the top of the salary scale.

✔ **Shoes:** Shoes should look businesslike and be dark coloured — no strappy shoes, sandals or mile-high stilettos.

✔ **Make-up:** Avoid wearing heavy make-up — on you or on your collar line.

✔ **Accessories:** Leave flashy or distracting jewellery — dangly ding-a-ling earrings, clunky bracelets, giant spiky rings that bruise fingers when shaking hands — at home in your jewellery box. And avoid chipped nail polish, if you wear it.

Nail polish gone wild

Should you sport any nail colour other than the classic reds and pinks at a job interview? How about blue, green, orange, purple or turquoise nail polish? So many women apply wild nail colours that this colour celebration once thought to be a passing fad has moved into mainstream acceptance. Good idea? Bad idea? Career coaches' opinions vary.

The 'No' answer: Stick with conservative colours, in case the hiring decider is a fuddy-duddy who hates trying new things or who considers the unconventional end of the colour palette to be in vulgar taste.

The 'Yes' answer: Ditch the sparkles and super-long nails, but don't leave wild colours to tweens, teens and twenty-somethings. Become an early adopter because it suggests that you lean forward to stay up with the times — a good strategy for the more mature set.

For *men*, a business casual checklist includes the following:

- ✔ **Clothing:** Don a casual jacket or blazer, especially navy blue, black or grey, with colour-coordinated long trousers or pressed khakis. Shirts should have collars, be long sleeved and stay tucked into pants; button-down shirts are good but not mandatory.

- ✔ **Shoes:** Choose dress shoes and a matching belt; loafers are acceptable.

- ✔ **Socks:** Wear dark socks that are mid-calf length.

- ✔ **Ties:** Choose simple (not too busy) ties for job interviews, unless you know from your research that a tie isn't part of the uniform where you're interviewing.

- ✔ **Accessories:** Limit jewellery to a conservative wristwatch.

Any interviewee, male or female, is better off steering clear of the following:

- ✔ Dark-tinted glasses and sunglasses atop your head or hanging in front of your collar

- ✔ Electronic devices (even on vibrate mode — the buzzing sound is annoying)

- ✔ Joke or fad watches

This advice is so important that it bears repeating: Advance research is the only way to be on sure footing. You're gambling if you assume that you know what business casual means in your interview setting — or even whether you should dress in business casual. When in doubt, scout it out.

Working in casual wear

True casual work attire is suitable for hands-on working men and women. Often a company uniform is required when you're on the job, but when you're in job interview mode, the main point to remember is to look neat and clean, with no holes or tears in your clothing. Colours and style don't matter as much as they do in conservative and business casual interview dressing, but your overall appearance does.

Don't let them smell you first

Grooming has a strong influence on hiring decisions. Who hasn't nearly passed out after smelling someone's salami breath? Who hasn't been revolted by rank body odour? Who hasn't been turned off by spinach flecks on teeth?

A recent National Association of Colleges and Employers survey reports a rejection of candidates who don't pass the sniff test. In fact, 73 per cent of respondents stated they don't want slovenly, smelly or dirt-ridden employees working anywhere on the premises. *Translation:* Shower. Brush. Comb. Clean is as clean smells.

Here's a short checklist for both men and women:

- ✔ **Clothing:** Shirts or quality knit tops and well-pressed pants are appropriate. Avoid wrinkled or soiled clothing, and don't wear T-shirts with writing on them.

- ✔ **Shoes:** Polished leather shoes or rubber-soled athletic shoes are fine. Just don't embarrass yourself by waltzing in wearing grungy sneakers.

- ✔ **Grooming:** Make 100-per-cent sure your hair and fingernails are neat and clean.

Selecting creative fashion

Most job seekers interview in attire suggesting that they're serious and centred in a business culture. But if you work in a creative environment, take fashion risks and go for artistry, design consciousness, innovation, trendiness, new styles and, yes, even whimsy.

You're probably way ahead of me and already follow high- and low-fashion statements online and in magazines like *Vogue, Marie Claire, Oyster, Lucire, GQ Australia* and *M2 New Zealand.* You know what they say about fashion: In one year and out the other. So I don't attempt to compile a checklist for either sex, because in a fashion-forward office, everything would be outdated by the time this book is published.

In offices where employees are encouraged to show originality, a reasonably creative look (not too far over the top) beats out conservative dress, and maybe business casual as well. It all depends on the company culture as seen through the hiring boss's eyes.

No worse for wear

When you've no budget to burn but need quality-looking interview wardrobe items, why not treasure-hunt in resale and opportunity shops? When you've no budget at all, seek free donated workplace clothing, which is available to help economically disadvantaged women acquire and keep jobs. Dress for Success (www.dressforsuccess.org) is a worldwide non-profit organisation with chapters in many Australian and New Zealand cities.

Fitted for Work (www.fitted forwork.org) is a not-for-profit Australian organisation for women that provides free business clothing as well as personal outfitting services. At the time of writing, they have offices in Melbourne and Sydney.

Men seeking free gently used work clothing can access services provided by charities such as the Society of St Vincent de Paul (www.vinnies. org.au and svdp.org.nz) and The Salvation Army (www. salvationarmy.org.au and www.salvationarmy.org.nz).

Chapter 9

Rehearse Away the Stage Fright

In This Chapter

▶ Staring down your jitters

▶ Making body language walk your talk

▶ Keeping in mind key pointers for all situations

▶ Being prepared for disruptions and awkward silences

▶ Practising ... and practising again

*Y*ou're nervous. You have a mouthful of 'ah' and 'um' cotton. You're a bundle of nerves, from shaking knees and clammy palms to racing pulse beats and tummy butterflies, as you make your appearance on an interview stage.

What you have is a galloping case of stage fright. Sound familiar? As the late great American newscaster Walter Cronkite remarked, 'It's natural to have butterflies. The secret is to get them to fly in formation.'

In this chapter, I cover how to beat stage fright through refocusing and rehearsing — and give you some tips on getting those butterflies to fly in formation.

Refocusing Attitude Can Calm Nerves

You're not alone in your nervousness. Most people — including me — start out with a case of the shakes when interviewing or making a speech. When I began giving speeches, I could feel my throat drying up as panic fried my memory banks. I knew I had to go out and orate to promote my media careers column, but doing so was not my idea of fun.

Then one day things changed. I was in Florida addressing a group of career counsellors when a teacher with whom I shared a podium watched me shake my way through my remarks. The teacher, herself an accomplished speaker, took me aside after the program and delivered one of the best pieces of advice I've ever been given. The teacher explained that nervousness is caused by the fear of looking ridiculous to others. She said:

> *When you are nervous, you are focusing on yourself. Try to focus on how you are helping other people by sharing with them the knowledge you've acquired.*
>
> *You've been privileged to gather information not many people have. Think about serving others, not about yourself when you're on stage.*

Her simple words of wisdom were an epiphany, a wake-up call. Thanks, Teach, for putting my nervousness into perspective.

How can *you* use that perspective? By realising that preparing for a job interview is not unlike preparing for a speech or theatrical performance.

Three steps to fright-free interviewing

Aim for a flawless performance by following three basic steps in your interview plan.

1. **Memorise your basic message.**

   Get your skills and competencies, accomplishments, and other qualifications down pat. Rehearse until you're comfortable answering questions and you've practised your basic presentation techniques. Rehearse until you know your self-marketing material cold.

2. **Personalise each self-marketing interview pitch.**

   Research each potential employer to customise your basic presentation for each job. Learn how to research each interviewing company in Chapter 5.

3. **Spotlight your audience.**

   Focus on how your talents can benefit your audience. Don't worry about how imperfect you may appear.

Making your audience the centre of attention goes a long way toward writing 'The End' to your nervousness.

More techniques to stop stressing out

When stars of the theatre walk on stage, they claim the stage from wing to wing, backdrop to footlights. With confidence and charisma, they win the audience's undivided interest. In a phrase, stars have stage presence. They are comfortable on stage.

Career coaches offer a variety of suggestions to get your butterflies flying like an air force jet, ranging from relaxation techniques to visualisation exercises. Here's a list of ideas that may be just what you need:

- ✔ **Deep breaths are an instant stress reliever.** Take a deep breath, breathing from your toes all the way through your body, and then slowly exhale. Repeat twice more, for three deep breaths in all.

- ✔ **Clench your fists.** Hold for three to five seconds. Release. Releasing your hands relaxes your shoulders and jaw. Repeat three times.

- ✔ **Push away anxiety.** Go into a nearby toilet and lean into a wall like a suspect being frisked in a cop show. Push hard, as though you want to push the wall down. Grunt as you push. Speech coaches say that when you push a wall and grunt, you contract certain muscles, which, in turn, reduces anxiety. Don't let anyone see you do this exercise, though — an observer may think you're loony tunes.

- ✔ **Visualise the outcome you want.** Top athletes often use visualisation techniques to calm jitters, improve concentration and boost athletic performance. They picture in their mind opponents' actions and strategy, and then picture themselves countering the manoeuvre.

  A golfer, for example, may run a movie in his head of where he wants the ball to go before he takes a swing. For an interview, you can visualise meeting the interviewer, answering and asking questions, closing the interview well (see Chapter 11) or even being offered the job on the spot.

- ✔ **Combine relaxation with visualisation.** Visualise a quiet, beautiful scene, such as a green valley filled with wildflowers or a soothing garden with a waterfall. Inhale and think 'I am.' Exhale and think, 'Calm.' Breathe at least 12 times. Next, recall a successful interview experience.

Rehearsing out loud

Practise speaking the messages you plan to deliver at your job interview — such as a listing of your five top skills, how you will answer questions (Chapters 14 to 19), and how you will ask questions (Chapter 10).

Why not just silently read your message statements over and over? Coaching experts say *rehearsing* information aloud helps fix content in your mind. Rehearsing your statements at least five times makes them yours.

Yes, that's a lot of repetition, but remember this: Rehearsing five times beats the time frame of a famous orator in ancient Greece. A dude named Demosthenes worked to improve his elocution by talking with pebbles in his mouth and reciting verses while running along the seashore over the roar of the waves. Supposedly Demosthenes also went into a cave to learn oratory skills.

Not having a watch, a calendar or a smartphone (and unable to use a sundial in a cave), Demosthenes shaved off the hair on half of his head and didn't come out until it grew back three months later. When he finally came out, listeners gladly lent him their ears because he had turned himself into the man with the golden tonsils.

Before an interview, free your mind of personal worries — like paying the mortgage or picking up your kid after school. When your personal concerns can't be handled immediately — and most can't — write them down and promise yourself that you'll deal with them after your job interview.

Unlock the Power of Body Language

Carol Kinsey Goman is one of the business world's foremost authorities on body language. An executive coach, popular author and keynote speaker, Dr Goman explains a phenomenon that you probably haven't thought much about: In a job interview, two conversations are going on at the same time.

The first conversation is the verbal one. But the second conversation, the nonverbal one, can seriously support or disastrously weaken your spoken words.

Fascinated, on behalf of job seekers everywhere, I interviewed Dr Goman. Here are my questions, followed by Dr Goman's answers:

How quickly does body language affect your interview?

Immediately! Starting with the first steps you take inside the interviewing room, interviewers make judgements about you within seconds. The precise number of seconds is debated by social psychologists and interviewing professionals — it's complicated.

But most researchers and first-impression observers agree that initially sizing you up requires mere seconds. In that wisp of time, decisions are made about your credibility, trustworthiness, warmth, empathy, confidence and competence.

While you can't stop people from making snap decisions — the human brain is hardwired in this way — you *can* understand how to make those decisions work in your favour.

What can you say in seconds, other than 'Hello'?

Obviously, you won't impress anyone by what you say in time measured by seconds. Instead, it's all about what you *don't* say. It's all about your body language.

But if you fail to score during the first impressionable seconds, can't you recover your chances later in the interview?

A poor first impression is hard to overcome, no matter how solid your credentials or impressive your resume.

So how can you do well in an interview from the get-go?

Here are powerful ways you can make a favourable first impression.

> ✔ **Command your attitude.** People pick up your attitude instantly. Think about the situation. Make a conscious choice about the attitude you want to communicate. Attitudes that attract people are friendly, cheerful, receptive, patient, approachable, welcoming, helpful and curious. Attitudes that deter people are angry, impatient, bored, arrogant, fearful, disheartened and distrustful.

✔ **Stand tall.** Your body language is a reflection of your emotions, but it also influences your emotions. Start projecting confidence and credibility by standing up straight, pulling your shoulders back and holding your head high. Just by assuming this physical position, you will begin to feel surer of yourself.

✔ **Smile.** A smile is an invitation, a sign of welcome. It says, 'I'm friendly and approachable.' Smiling influences how other people respond.

The human brain prefers happy faces, recognising them more quickly than those with negative expressions. Research shows that when you smile at someone, the smile activates that person's reward centre. It's a natural response for the other person to smile back at you.

✔ **Make eye contact.** Looking at someone's eyes transmits energy and indicates interest and openness. A simple way to improve your eye contact in those first few seconds is to look into the interviewer's eyes long enough to notice what colour they are. With this one simple technique, you will dramatically increase your likeability factor.

If you feel uncomfortable looking into an interviewer's eyes too long, look the interviewer squarely in the nose and you appear to be making eye contact. You communicate openness and honesty.

Caveat: Although good eye contact is excellent body language, don't try for a laser lock on the interviewer. Imagine two cats in a staring contest — in the Animal Kingdom, nobody moves until somebody swats. Break the tension by periodically looking away.

✔ **Raise your eyebrows.** Open your eyes slightly more than normal to simulate the 'eyebrow flash' that is the universal signal of recognition and acknowledgement.

✔ **Lean in slightly.** Leaning forward with the small of your back against the chair shows you're engaged and interested. We naturally lean toward people and things we like or agree with. But be respectful of the other person's space.

✔ **Shake hands.** This is the quickest way to establish rapport. It's also the most effective. Research confirms that it takes an average of three hours of continuous interaction to develop the same level of rapport that you can get with a single handshake.

But make sure you keep your body squared off to the other person, facing the person fully. Use a firm — but not bone-crushing — grip with palm-to-palm contact. And hold the other person's hand a few fractions of a second longer than you are naturally inclined to do. This action conveys additional sincerity and quite literally 'holds' the other person's attention while you exchange greetings.

What are some of the top flops in body language?

Avoid signs that indicate nervousness, submission, or weakness, such as the following:

- ✔ **Projecting agitation:** Try not to fidget or change positions frequently. Don't bounce your legs, lock your ankles or rock from side to side. Don't dart your eyes, blink in slow motion, or blink abnormally fast. Never wave your arms with hands over your head to make a point because it implies that you're out of control.

- ✔ **Looking uninterested:** Overcome any tendency to cross your arms, which suggests disagreement or disbelief, especially when leaning back. Avoid continually bowing your head, as though you are saying, 'I have no idea of the right answer' or 'Poor me'.

- ✔ **Seeming unsure:** Standing with your feet close together can make you seem timid. (Widen your stance, relax your knees, and centre your weight in your lower body, to look more 'solid' and sure of yourself.) Avoid hanging on to your laptop, purse or briefcase as though it was toddler Linus's security blanket in the Charlie Brown comics.

- ✔ **Appearing tired:** Slumping in the chair is a really bad idea. 'Slacker' is the first thing that comes to mind if you're a member of Gen Y or Gen X, and 'old timer' arises if you're a boomer.

- ✔ **Suggesting arrogance:** A nonverbal signal of confidence is holding your head up. But if you tilt your head back even slightly, the signal changes to one of looking down your nose at the interviewer or job being discussed. Snooty.

Learn your best moves in living colour

Reinforce your new understanding of communicating nonverbally through gestures and movements by viewing the five-star videos on body language expert Dr Goman's website, www. nonverbaladvantage.com. They're short and they're free.

Stage Directions for All Players

As you rehearse your interviewing presentation, aim for the A-list of candidates by heeding the following hints:

- ✔ Practise focusing your discussion on the employer's needs. Show that you understand those needs, that you possess the specific skills to handle the job, and that you are in sync with the company culture.

- ✔ Don't discuss previous employment rejections — you come off as a constant audition reject.

- ✔ Develop and practise justifiably proud statements of your accomplishments — that is, those that directly relate to the job you want.

- ✔ Practise descriptions of your leadership qualities and initiative, and remember to express them *in context* of what you accomplished. (Did you lead 10 people, 100 people or 1,000 people? What was the result? Has anyone in the company accomplished the same thing?)

- ✔ It's okay to admit a misstep. If pressed, you can fess up to a goof you've made in your career. But rehearse satisfying explanations of how you learned from your one mistake — or two or three. And try not to laugh while you're admitting that you're human.

- ✔ Don't practise long monologues — be fair: Split air time with your interviewer.

Different strokes for different folks

Interviewing coaches say a winning role-related voice and head tilts vary as much as appropriate dress codes for Oscar performances. Some examples include the following.

When applying for a service job: You'll seem more personable by slightly tilting up your chin and letting your voice rise by a hair at the end of each key sentence.

When applying for a management job: You'll come across as more boss-like by using a steady, calm and confident voice as you keep your chin level.

Anticipating Interview Trapdoors

No matter how well you're doing as you sail through an interview, certain things can throw you off balance when you're not forewarned. Rehearse in your mind how you would handle the situations in the following sections.

Disruptions

As you rehearse, keep in mind that not everything that happens during the interview is related to you. Your meeting may be interrupted by a ringing phone, the interviewer's co-workers or even the interviewer's emergency needs. Add the factor of interview interference to your mock drills.

Because the show must go on, find language to politely overlook these interruptions with patient concentration. Practise keeping a tab on what you're discussing between disruptions, in case the interviewer doesn't.

Silent treatment

Interviewers sometimes use silence strategically. Moments of silence are intended to get candidates to answer questions more fully — and even to get them to blurt out harmful information they had no intention of revealing.

Instead of concentrating on your discomfort during these silences, recognise the technique. Either wait out the silence until the interviewer speaks or fill it with a well-chosen question (see Chapter 10) that you have tucked up your sleeve. Don't bite on the silent treatment ploy, panic and spill information that doesn't advance your cause. Don't run your mouth for no reason.

Turning the tables, you can use your own silence strategy to encourage the interviewer to elaborate or to show that you're carefully considering issues under discussion.

Take One ... Take Two ... Take Three ...

Practise your scenes until they feel right, until they feel spontaneous. Rehearsing gives you the power to become a confident communicator with the gift of presence. No more nervousness, no more zoning out. No more undercutting body language. Your butterflies fly in formation.

Tell me why I care

'So what?' 'Who cares?' 'What good does your past accomplishment do me?' This kind of question may be unspoken, but it's lying in ambush deep in every employer's mind. Each time you mention a previous job duty or accomplishment, pretend the employer is really thinking, What does this all mean for my benefit? Will it make money? Save money? Grow my company's market reach? What? Tell me why I care. Rehearse telling me why I care and make the sale!

Chapter 10

Looking Good with Questions You Ask

- -

In This Chapter

▶ Asking work questions before the offer

▶ Asking personal questions after the offer

▶ Building your confidence and smoking out hidden objections

▶ Treading lightly around delicate questions

▶ Finishing with the right question

- -

*S*o you just finished answering a seemingly endless line of questions about your work history and your education, and you're pretty confident that you held your own. Now the interviewer turns to you and asks, 'Do you have any questions?' This question is your cue to ask how much money you're gonna make at this outfit, right? Wrong!

In this chapter, I cover one of the least understood parts of the interview — the types of questions you ask and when you ask them. Your questions offer major chances for garnering curtain calls or being booed off the stage. Sort your question opportunities into two categories:

✔ **Questions that sell you:** These questions help you get an offer; they're a way to sell without selling.

✔ **Questions that address your personal agenda:** These questions about pay, benefits and other self-interest items need to be asked only after you receive an offer — or at least a heavy hint of an offer.

Asking Selling Questions before the Offer

For all jobs, asking about anything other than work issues before a hiring offer comes your way is a serious strategic error. The interviewer, particularly a hiring manager who resents the time 'diverted' from typical duties to an interview, is totally uninterested in your needs at this point.

What's important to the interviewer is solving the hiring problem. *First we decide, then we deal* — that's the thinking.

To talk about your needs before an offer turns the interviewer's mind to negative thoughts: All you want is money, leave entitlements and a nice holiday on the company. You're not interested in doing the job.

Keep your focus on the employer's needs and how you can meet them. Sell yourself by asking questions that are

- ✔ Work focused
- ✔ Task focused
- ✔ Function focused

Ask about the position's duties and challenges. Ask what outcomes you're expected to produce. Ask how the position fits into the department and the department into the company. Ask about typical assignments. Here are examples of work-related questions:

- ✔ What would be my first project if I were hired for this position?
- ✔ What would my key responsibilities be?
- ✔ Who (and how many) would I supervise? To whom would I report?
- ✔ Would I be working as a member of a team?
- ✔ What percentage of time would I spend communicating with customers, co-workers and managers?

- ✔ Would on-the-job training be required for a new product?

- ✔ Can you describe a typical day?

- ✔ If I produced double my quota, would you double my base pay? (Although this is best left until the second interview.)

- ✔ Was the last person in this job promoted? What's the potential for promotion?

- ✔ How would you describe the atmosphere here? Formal and traditional? Energetically informal?

- ✔ Where is the company headed? Merger? Growth?

- ✔ What type of training would I receive?

- ✔ What resources would I have to do the job?

- ✔ How much would I travel, if any?

- ✔ (If a contract job) Do you anticipate extensive overtime to finish the project on schedule?

- ✔ Where does this position fit into the company's organisational structure?

- ✔ What results would you expect from my efforts and on what timetable? What improvements need to be made on how the job has been done until now?

How much time should you invest in asking selling questions? Five to ten minutes is not too much. Gregory J Walling, a top US executive recruiter, says he's never heard an employer complain about a candidate being too interested in work.

Don't ask questions about information you can glean from research. Portraying yourself as an A-list candidate and then asking 'lazy questions' dims your star power. Lazy questions would be something like 'Is this the only office you have in Australia [or New Zealand]?', 'Who is the CEO of this company?' or 'What products or services do you offer?' Make sure you have browsed through the employer's website and any other information that is publicly available to ensure you don't ask a question you should know the answer to. (Refer to Chapter 5 for more on researching before an interview.)

Asking Self-Interest Questions after the Offer

When you have the offer, you're ready to make the switch from giving to receiving information. I discuss negotiating salary and benefits in Chapter 7, but you'll also want to know about information like overtime, flexitime, rostered days off (RDOs), frequency of performance reviews and (if it's a contract job) how long the job will last.

Although asking personal agenda questions in advance of an offer is unwise, after the offer, scoop up details of interest, such as these examples:

- ✔ Is my future relocation a possibility?

- ✔ Is my employee parking included in the offer?

- ✔ Does management delegate decision-making to others, or does it micromanage and require that I get approval of even the tiniest details?

- ✔ Where would I work in the building? Can I take a quick look at the location?

- ✔ Is the schedule fixed (such as 9 am to 5 pm) or flexible (my choice of hours)?

- ✔ Would I be paid overtime or be able to take it as time in lieu?

Ask with confidence

Be aware of how you phrase questions. Ask 'what would' questions that presume you'll be offered the job ('What would my key responsibilities be?' not 'What are the job's key responsibilities?').

Presumption phrasing shows self-confidence and subtly encourages the interviewer to visualise you in the position.

Drawing Out Hidden Objections

The questions you ask have one more mission: They're a good way to smoke out hidden concerns or objections that may keep you from finishing first in the competition.

Reasons that employers hang back with unspoken anxieties often relate to legal vulnerability (see Chapter 19 on inappropriate questions), or the interviewer may simply be uncomfortable asking about them.

Whatever the reason, silent concerns are hurdles standing in the way of your getting the job. Before the interview is over, you need to find a way to address any thorny issues and overcome them.

Good salespeople call techniques that do this 'drawing out objections'. Once you know the issues that — under the surface — are chilling your chances, try calling them out.

One of the best questions I've ever heard to jar loose unspoken doubts was passed on by legendary recruiting authority and author John Lucht (www.ritesite.com). When the interview is about four-fifths complete, Lucht suggests you ask this question: *What do you think would be the biggest challenge for someone with my background coming into this position?*

Here's your golden opportunity to bury any concerns on the spot or in your thank you letter. (If you can't collect your thoughts quickly enough, at least you'll have a clue for your next interview once you know what may be holding back employers from choosing you.)

Another tactic to control a problem lurking below the surface is to introduce it head-on and tell the employer what you want known about the situation. Here's an example of easing an interviewer's hidden concerns by bringing up a legally risky topic:

> *In your place, I'd probably be wondering how my children are cared for during the day. I may be concerned that I'd miss work should they become ill. Let me explain my very reliable childcare arrangements to you . . .*

Critics pan show-offs

I noticed in subsection 3.a of the government contractor's manual I.2.A, concerning future plans, that you squared the round table, using your supercomputer's component play box, and found that your sandbox is 95 per cent superior to the market's. Does this mean you plan to circle an outer galaxy and return to Earth on Greenwich Mean Time?

Huh? Research is essential, but guard against flaunting your newly found knowledge with questions that would have given Einstein a little headache. Interviewers interpret these questions as a transparent bid to look smart.

But, you ask, shouldn't you look 'smart' at an interview? Yes. Just don't cross the fine line that exists between being well researched and fully prepared for an interview, and trying to be a *nouveau omniscient*. (Don't you love that term? I looked it up. It means newly informed know-it-all.)

Showing off is a quality that causes otherwise charming, bright, gregarious and attractive people to be turned down. It's just not a likeable trait. If you don't have a good handle on what is and what isn't showing off, maybe a friend can help you work on that distinction.

After hidden objections see daylight, you have a chance to shoo away elephants in the room that are standing between you and a job offer.

Asking Certain Questions Very Carefully

Handle questions to potential employers about their own performance with great tact — especially when a Millennium-generation candidate asks them of a Boomer-generation boss. Proceed with caution into territory like the following:

- How would you describe your management style?
- Do your employees admire you as a boss?

Although you need as much information as possible to make good job choices, asking a potential boss these kinds of questions in the wrong tone of voice may make you seem way too audacious. Moreover, direct questions about personal characteristics and values tend to elicit pure topspin.

Instead, ask questions designed to draw out companywide anecdotal answers:

- ✔ How did the company handle a recent downsizing?
- ✔ How did managers react to someone who took a stand on principle?
- ✔ Who are the company's heroes?

This approach encourages conversation that can be very informative. Questions are tools. Use them wisely.

Ending Suspense by Asking the Right Question

In Chapter 11 you can find a line-up of fundamental questions to ask at the end of each interview. Want another option for immediate feedback? When your meeting has sailed smoothly along and you want to know your odds right now but you don't want to appear overconfident or too anxious, ask the right question:

> *Should I assume you'd like me to continue in the interviewing process?*
>
> *[yes] What would the next step be?*
>
> *[no] I'm sorry to hear that. Can you tell me why I won't be in the running? (If you can overcome the objections, give it a try; if not, thank the interviewer for the time spent with you and move on.)*

When you don't hear the *yes* word, at least you won't be holding your breath to know whether this particular work opportunity is a lost cause. If the *no* word sparks a serious state of doldrums, break out an effective mood elevator — hot fudge sundae? funny movie? upbeat music?

Chapter 11

Leaving a Good Impression

. . . .

In This Chapter

▶ Closing an interview like a pro

▶ Pursuing the job without being a pest

▶ Winning with a thanks/marketing letter

▶ Following up the interview

▶ Improving interviews with a post-interview checklist

. . . .

Curtain call time! You sense that it's almost the moment to go. The interview seems to be winding down. In most instances, a job offer doesn't come at this point.

How can you be sure the interview is almost over? Watch for these nonverbal clues: The interviewer may begin shuffling papers, glancing at a wall clock or watch, stretching silences, and perhaps standing up. Then you hear words that confirm your hunch:

> ✔ *Thanks for coming in. We'll be interviewing more candidates through the next week or so. After that, I'll probably get back to you about a second interview.*

> ✔ *Thanks for talking with me. I think your qualifications make you a definite candidate for this position. When I'm done with all the initial interviews, I'll get back to you.*

> ✔ *All your input has been really helpful. Now that I know everything I need to know about you, do you have any questions about the company or the position?* (Careful — ask only job-related questions — you don't have the offer yet; refer to Chapter 10.)

In this chapter, I cue your best exit lines and remind you to exhibit friendly confidence, no matter how the interviewer behaves.

Making a Strategic Exit

Do yourself a favour by never leaving a job interview empty-handed. Rather than quietly fading into history, memorise these four important points:

- ✔ Immerse your departure in *interactive selling*. Sales professionals use this term to mean a great deal of back and forth, give and take, and questions and answers.

- ✔ Reprise your qualifications and the benefits you bring to the job. You're a great match and a wonderful fit, and you'll be quickly productive.

- ✔ Find out what happens next in the hiring process. Mysteries are for crime show viewers.

- ✔ Prop open the door for your follow-up. Without paving the way, you may seem desperate when you call back to see what's up.

Your parting sales pitch

Haven't you sold yourself enough during this Show Stopper interview? Yes and no. People — including interviewers — often forget what they hear. Start your close with another chorus of your five best skills. (See Chapter 17 for answers to the question, 'Why should I hire you?'.) Then ask

> Do you see any gaps between my qualifications and the requirements for the job?

> Based on what we've discussed today, do you have any concerns about my ability to do well in this job? Any reservations about hiring me?

You're looking for gaps and hidden objections so that you can make them seem insignificant. But if the gaps aren't wide and the objections not lethal to your candidacy, attempt to overcome stated shortcomings. You can make this attempt based on what you found out in your earlier research. Here's an effective formula you can use to *engage the interviewer*:

1. **Sell your qualifications (skills and other requirements for the job).**

2. **Ask for objections.**

3. **Listen carefully.**

4. **Overcome objections.**

5. **Restate your qualifications (using different words).**

After you restate your qualifications, you may find the time is ripe to reaffirm your interest in the job and subtly lead toward an offer. Here's one example to illustrate how such a scenario might play out:

> *I hope I've answered your concerns on the X issue. Do you have further questions or issues about my background, qualifications or anything else at this point? This job and I sound like a terrific match.*

Depending upon the interviewer's response, make your move:

> *I hope you agree that this position has my name on it. As I understand, your position requires X, and I can deliver X; your position requires Y, and I can deliver Y; your position requires Z, and I can deliver Z.*

> *So there seems to be a good match here! Don't you think so?*

> *I'm really glad I had the chance to talk with you. I know that with what I learned at [Violet Tech] when I [established its internet website], I can [set up an excellent website for you, too].*

Leaving the door open

How can you prop the door open for a follow-up? You seek the interviewer's permission to call back; with permission, you won't seem intrusive. Use these statements as models to gain the permission:

> *What's the next step in the hiring process, and when do you expect to make a decision? (You're trying to get a sense of the timetable.)*

> *I'm quite enthusiastic about this position. When and how do we take the next step?*

> *May I call if I have further questions? Or would you prefer that I email or text you?*

I know you're not done reviewing candidates; when can I reach you to check up on the progress of your search?

I understand you'll call me back after you've seen every candidate for this position; would you mind if I call you for an update or if I have more questions?

I appreciate the time you spent with me; I know you're going to be really busy recruiting, so when can I call you?

I look forward to that second interview you mentioned — can I call you later to schedule it after my work hours so I don't have to throw off my current employer's schedule?

You say I'm the leading candidate for this position. Terrific! That's great to hear —when shall we talk again?

In the final moments, be certain to express thanks to the interviewer for the time spent with you. Say it with a smile, eye-to-nose, and a firm but gentle handshake: *This position looks like a terrific opportunity and a great fit for me — I look forward to hearing from you.* Then leave. Don't linger.

As soon as you're alone at a place where you can make notes, write a summary of the meeting. Concentrate especially on material for your follow-up moves, described later in this chapter.

How Hard Should You Sell?

How hard you should sell and how eager you should be depends on such things as age, critical experience and the level of the job you're seeking. No behaviour is perfect for every candidate and every situation.

When you're in a sales field, are just starting out, lack experience in a job's requirements or aren't obviously superior to your competition, don't hold back on selling your advantages or showing your enthusiasm.

When you have relevant experience and offer in-demand skills, or are being considered for a senior-level job, allow yourself to be wooed a bit. You don't want to be seen as jumping at every opportunity. It's the old story: The more anxious you seem, the less money you're offered.

Recruiters follow up for you

You don't have to follow up with the employer when you were introduced to the company by a third-party recruiter — the recruiter follows up for you, negotiating the offer or accepting the turndown. You can get a report card from your recruiter fairly quickly.

When the gap between your qualifications and the job's requirements is the size of Bass Strait, accept the fact that the job will go to someone else. Suppose, for instance, that the position requires five years' experience, including two years of supervisory experience. You thought you could talk your way through the gap with your three years of total experience and no years of supervisory experience. Fat chance!

When you just don't have the chops for the position, salvage your time and effort by acknowledging that although you may not be ideal for this particular position, interviewing for it has caused you to admire the company and its people. You'd appreciate being contacted if a better match comes along.

Follow Up or Fall Behind

What takes place after the first selection interview — when candidates are ranked — decides who has the inside track on winning the job.

Your follow-up may be the tiebreaker that gives you the win over other promising candidates. And even if the employer already planned to offer you the job, your follow-up creates goodwill that kick-starts your success when you join the company.

Follow up vigorously. It's your caring that counts.

Your basic tools are emails and other media, telephone calls and referees.

Email

In this digital age, an email follow-up thank you is fine for most jobs. But your email should really be a persuasive self-marketing communication masquerading as a thank you email, because this makes interviewers more likely to pay attention to you as a thoughtful and conscientious top contender.

In constructing a thanks/marketing email that actually does you some good, use the same powerful concepts you would employ for a targeted resume that directly matches your qualifications with the job's requirements. (Check out *Writing Resumes & Cover Letters For Dummies*, 2nd Australian and New Zealand Edition, Wiley, for more.)

Get started with the following content capsules for your thanks/marketing email aimed at converting your candidacy into a job offer:

- ✔ Express appreciation for the interviewer's time and for giving you a fresh update on the organisation's immediate direction.

- ✔ Remind the interviewer of what specifically you can do for a company, not what a company can do for you. As you did in closing your interview, draw verbal links between a company's immediate needs and your qualifications.

- ✔ Repeat your experience in handling concerns that were discussed during the interview.

- ✔ Tie up loose ends by adding information to a question you didn't handle well during the interview.

- ✔ Overcome objections the interviewer expressed about offering you the job. For example, if the job has an international component and the interviewer was concerned that you've never worked in Asia, explain that you've worked productively in other cultures, notably Australia (if you're from New Zealand) or vice versa.

- ✔ Reaffirm your interest in the position and respect for the company.

Consider these observations on communicating after an interview by email:

- ✔ Email is more conversational and easier for a quick reply. On the other hand, it's also easier to say *no* in an email message than on the telephone.

- ✔ Use email if that's the way you sent your resume and especially if the employer requested electronic communication in a job ad.

- ✔ Use email when you're dealing with a high-tech firm; the firm's hiring authority probably doesn't remember what paper is and may think voicemail is a bother.

Don't make blanket assumptions about whether spam filters will prevent your message from reaching the interviewer. Instead, ask the interviewer or a receptionist in advance about the best way to send an email message.

If you feel a letter would be more appropriate than an email, the content for a thank you letter need not differ much, if at all, from that of an email. You may expand on some of your points in a letter, but make sure you keep it to no more than two pages.

Other digital media

Newer media tools — chiefly the casual communication of *texting*, *instant messaging* and *social networking* — have jumped into the job search, mostly driven by younger generations. Reports so far suggest an age-based cultural divide on short-form messages. What about employer acceptance of thank you messages after an interview?

Hiring professionals are frowning at such quickie and lax communication — everything from sending an SMS message to a recruiter after an interview in texting lingo, to adding the interviewer as a friend on Facebook. They consider such throwaway thanks disrespectful.

Another new idea — creating a 30-second *video email* to send interview thanks to a hiring professional — doesn't have a track record yet. But I can see how it could be a fresh tool to stand out from the crowd. Using search terms such as 'video email', 'vid mail', 'video messaging' and 'vmail', browse for services that provide this option; add the year of your inquiry to your search.

Telephone calls

Once upon a time, all that job seekers had to worry about when calling about potential employment was getting past gatekeepers. They solved that problem in various ways, by adopting a pleasant and honest manner and making an ally of the assistant by revealing the refreshing truth about why they're calling, as one example.

Some job seekers battled back by trying to reach the interviewer before 8:30 am or after 5:30 pm, when the assistant wasn't likely to be on deck and the interviewer alone would pick up the phone.

Those were the good old days. Now voicemail has joined gatekeepers in throwing huge roadblocks in front of job seekers who try to follow up on interviews.

The big voicemail question for job seekers is whether to leave a message on voicemail. Opinions vary but, as a practical matter, you may have to leave a message if you don't connect after the first few calls. All your calls won't be returned, but your chances improve when you say something interesting in a 30-second sound bite:

> *This is [your name]. I'm calling about the [job title or department] opening. After reflecting on some of the issues you mentioned during our meeting, I thought of a solution for one problem you might like to know. My number is ____.*

Opening the conversation

Here's a sprinkling of conversation starters:

- *Is this a good time to talk?*

- *I understand you're still reviewing many applications, but ...*

- *I forgot to go into the key details of (something mentioned during the interview) that may be important to you.*

- *While listening to you, I neglected to mention my experience in (function). It was too important for me to leave out, since the position calls for substantial background in that area.*

- *I appreciate your emphasis on ____.*

Keeping the conversational ball rolling

Try these approaches to maintain the conversation:

- Remind the interviewer of why you're so special and what makes you unique (exceptional work in a specific situation, innovating).

    Let me review what I'm offering you that's special.

- Establish a common denominator — a work or business philosophy.

    It seems like we both approach work in the [name of] industry from the same angle.

- Note a shared interest that benefits the employer.

    I found a new website that may interest you — it's [XYZ]. It reports on the news items we discussed ... Would you like the URL?

Priming your referees

Referees can make all the difference. Spend adequate time choosing and preparing the people who give you glowing testimonials. What they say about you is more convincing than what you say about yourself.

Call your referees and fill them in on your interview:

> *I had an interview today with [person, company]. We talked about the position, and it sounds like a perfect match for me. They wanted [give a list of key requirements], and that's just what I can supply.*

> *For instance, I have all this experience [match five key requirements with five of your qualifications] from when I worked with [name of company].*

> *Would you like me to email you those points I just mentioned? ... I was so happy about the interview I just wanted to thank you once more for all your help and support. I couldn't have done it without you.*

When you get a job offer at the interview

With an offer is on the table, bring up your self-interest (leave, bonuses, work hours) requests for information. Whip out a note pad and say,

I'm excited and grateful for your interest. I'd like to clear up just a few issues. Can you tell me about —?

Unless the circumstances are unusual, accepting or rejecting a job offer on the spot is not in your best interest. You're likely to think of something later that you forgot to negotiate. Improving an offer after you have accepted is difficult.

'Don't give referee details to anyone unless they're ready to offer you a job you'll accept,' advises John Lucht, author of the bible of executive job hunting, *Rites of Passage at $100,000 to $1 million+: Your Insider's Lifetime Guide to Executive Job-Changing and Faster Career Progress in the 21st Century* (Viceroy Press).

Lucht says the first time referees are contacted, they put on their best performance. He explains what happens next: 'The second time, they're a bit more hurried and perfunctory. As that sequence lengthens, they'll become less enthusiastic and begin to wonder why, if you're as good as they originally thought, are you still repeatedly referenced and not hired?'

Your After-Interview Checklist

Experts in any field become experts because they've made more mistakes than the rest of us. After your interview, take a few minutes to rate your performance. The following checklist can help you curb bad habits and become an expert at job interviewing:

- ✔ Were you on time?
- ✔ Did you use storytelling, examples, results and measurement of achievements to back up your claims and convince the questioner that you have the skills to do the job?

✔ Did you display high energy? Flexibility? Interest in learning new things?

✔ Did the opening of the interview go smoothly?

✔ Did you frequently make a strong connection between the job's requirements and your qualifications?

✔ Was your personal grooming immaculate? Were you dressed like company employees?

✔ Did you forget any important selling points? If so, did you put them in a follow-up email, letter or call-back?

✔ Did you smile? Did you make eye contact? Was your handshake good?

✔ Did you convey at least five major qualities the interviewer should remember about you?

✔ Did you make clear your understanding of the work involved in the job?

✔ Did you use enthusiasm and motivation to indicate that you're willing to do the job?

✔ Did you find some common ground to establish that you'll fit well into the company?

✔ Did you take the interviewer's cues to wrap it up?

✔ Did you find out the next step and leave the door open for your follow-up?

✔ After the interview, did you write down names and points discussed?

✔ What did you do or say that the interviewer obviously liked?

✔ Did you hijack the interview by grabbing control or speaking too much (more than half the time)?

✔ Would you have done something differently if you could redo the interview?

Please stay. We're not kidding.

Employers sometimes make counter-offers when a valued employee quits to take a better job. If you find yourself being wooed back, it's usually best to leave the counteroffer on the table, say thanks, and move on. Here's why:

- When substantial financial considerations aren't in the mix, most people leave a job because of a personality rift, blocked advancement or boring work. A generous counteroffer doesn't fix any of these things.

- After you've announced a departure, count yourself out of the inner circle. You won't be trusted as before.

- Renewing your enthusiasm will be challenging: You already know why you want to find the exit. If your current employer wouldn't promote you or give you a decent raise before you put on your walking shoes, don't expect anything different when it's time to move up to your next career level.

- If a recruiter connected you with the new offer and you say *yes* and then *no*, your credibility goes up in smoke — a negative that can come back to haunt you.

Onward and Upward

You've done it all — turned in a Show Stopper performance at your interview and followed up like a pro. Keep following up until you get another job or until you're told you aren't a good match for the position — or that while your qualifications were good, another candidate's were better.

Even then, write yet one more thank you/self-marketing email or letter, expressing your hope that you may work together in the future. Sometimes the first choice declines the job offer, and the employer moves on to the next name — perhaps yours.

Feedback when you're not offered the part

Disappointed job seekers often ask interviewers for reasons they weren't selected and for tips on how to do better in the future. Don't waste your time: You almost never will be given the real reason. Employers have no legal or ethical obligation to explain why you weren't the one. Instead, they're likely to offer these kinds of useless rationales: 'We didn't feel you were the best fit for this job' or 'We chose another candidate who had more experience' or 'Company policy won't allow me to comment.'

Why won't interviewers share the truth? Here are some of the reasons:

✔ **Legal exposure:** Companies are wary of lawsuits accusing them of discrimination. The less said, the less to be sued about.

✔ **Fast-paced world:** There's no profit in wasting prime hours on a dead end.

✔ **Discomfort factor:** Managers dislike giving negative feedback.

✔ **Scant information:** Human resources interviewers may not have enough details from hiring managers to give helpful answers, even if they were inclined to do so.

When you're not offered the part, review the After-Interview Checklist in this chapter. If you have the requisite qualifications and your performance doesn't need pumping up, the reason you didn't get an offer may have nothing to do with you. Square your shoulders for the next interview.

Part III
Presenting Yourself as the Best Candidate

Five Ways for Older Interviewees to Beat the 'Overqualified' Excuse

- ✔ **Clarify the interviewer's concerns:** Try to find out whether the interviewer really thinks you're overqualified — or just overaged — and whether you'll want to earn too much money or be bored by the position.

- ✔ **Enthusiastically address the interviewer's concerns, emphasising the positive:** Explain how you can grow in this position — today a clerk, tomorrow a back-up manager.

- ✔ **Show how you can use your experience to benefit the company:** This could be in solving long-term problems, building profit or assisting in other departments.

- ✔ **Make sure that the interviewer understands your qualifications:** Check whether you can quickly run through the training you've received during your career.

- ✔ **Explain how you're an anchor:** Particularly in an office full of younger people, present yourself as experienced, calm, stable and reliable. You can provide continuity.

Check out a free online article about interview responses for when you're changing careers at www.dummies.com/extras/successfuljobinterviewsau.

In this part . . .

- ✔ Highlight what you will bring to a company as a school leaver or recent graduate.

- ✔ Address the age issue if you're an older applicant and counter some of the most common objections and assumptions.

Chapter 12

Interviewing Tips for School Leavers and Graduates

• •

In This Chapter

▶ Understanding the common objections employers may have

▶ Recognising the benefits of the youngest generation of workers

▶ Sharing key tips for recent school and vocational college leavers and university graduates

▶ Scripting effective rookie interview answers

• •

*H*i there, recent school or vocational college leavers, or university graduates! You're part of a huge generation that's movin' on up to run the workplace show in the foreseeable future.

Researchers tag you as a new breed of techno-savvy worker. They say that you're early adopters who are constantly hooked up to multiple devices in order to know who and what you need to know. You text, you tweet, you post on social media. You are connected to the world!

But wait ... although they acknowledge the blessings of your magnificent digital sophistication, today's employers aren't ready to say all is well with your generation as workers, you self-indulgent young rascals, you.

So in this chapter, I help you discover some of the benefits and skills you can bring to the modern workplace, so you can highlight them for interviewers, and provide some tips and scripts to help you overcome common objections.

Playing Against Type: Busting the Stereotypes

They who still call the shots — in other words, employers and the people likely to interview you — are highly critical of behaviour like this:

- ✔ You show up for work in an outfit that exposes a tattoo or laugh at a joke to reveal a tongue piercing.

- ✔ They find you audaciously texting senior managers with requests about issues that should be handled with an immediate supervisor.

- ✔ They see you whipping out a smartphone and wasting time on the company clock.

To further illustrate the problems employers report about younger workers, I offer this fictional but representative snippet of a job interview:

> *Management consulting firm interviewer:* Would you like to know more about our company's quantitative analysis group?
>
> *Millennial professional:* As I have a master's degree, would I start as a senior analyst instead of just an analyst? What is the salary? How soon would I be eligible for a raise? When would I be considered for a promotion? Would I have to work past 5 pm? I need time off every January because I always go to Queensland then. Can I work flexibly to get half-day Fridays? I have a holiday house down the coast and like to get away before the traffic.

Admittedly, we're talking generational stereotypes here — certainly, no specific traits define an entire generation — but in job interviews, stereotypical criticism sometimes lurks but remains unspoken.

As a techno-savvy, well-educated person, you know you have to recognise a problem to fix it. In this chapter, I show you how to counter harmful youth-bashing stereotypes.

Beating a Bad Rap on Work Ethic

As a recent school leaver or university graduate, your *ability* to do the work that a job requires isn't so much in question. The iffy factor is your *willingness* to do the work in a manner an employer prefers.

While the work-ethic gripe isn't singular to the younger crowd (Gen X members used to hear the same complaints when they were your age), it hits your generation the hardest. Here's what critics say about people in their late teens or 20s:

- You have an attitude toward work that looks like laziness-meets-impatience.

- You often had to overachieve to get through competitive school, college or university admissions processes, so you don't feel particularly inclined to pay your dues.

- You make up the most pampered generation in history; you were expected to spend your spare time on extracurricular activities, not working part-time at the local fast-food restaurant.

- You're likely to look at a job interview in the way one 20-year-old candidate described it to a recruiter: 'a two-way conversation where the company puts out what they want and expect from me, and I put out what I want and expect from the company.'

- You're more demanding than previous generations and quick to focus attention on getting your own needs met rather than meeting the needs of your team.

- You can't think on your feet. You don't work well alone, maybe because you grew up on a steady stream of organised sports and other team or teacher-led activities. You're comfortable only when pursuing well-defined goals as part of a team and can't solve problems independently. (Mum, Dad, help!)

Today's rookies are too often stereotyped as refusing to pay their dues, slacking off, holding unrealistic expectations, being unwilling to work hard or long, and being limited in the ability to make independent decisions and solve problems. Nevertheless, if you don't meet the generalisation head on, it can cause you to miss out on a job you want.

The positive performance you give during an interview dispelling the poor-work-ethic stereotyping can erase doubts about your willingness to do a job. Listen closely without interrupting and resist the temptation to punctuate sentences with words like 'exactly', as if you knew all that information the recruiter or employer has just told you way before they opened their mouth.

Tips for School Leavers and Graduates

Concentrating on the skills and accomplishments you provide and on what you bring to the employer — not what you want from the job — goes a long way toward wiping out unspoken concerns that chill job offers. Here are more tips for combating misperceptions:

- **Show perspective.** Every generation believes it's substantially different from those who have gone before and, therefore, deserves a pass to rewrite the rules. That's true only in the methods and technology used to make one's way in life.

  As scholar and publisher of Impact Books, Dr Ron Krannich (www.impactpublications.com) says, 'Despite a trendy Generation Y designation, today's college graduates still must learn to connect with the right people who can hire them for good jobs, showing they can add value to the organisations they want to join.'

- **Be confident.** But don't be a prancing pony in your interviewing persona, confusing attitude with confidence. Try to come across as able but eager to learn. Radiating arrogance that implies the workplace rules must bend to accommodate your preferences because you're young and techno savvy won't play well with older bosses who have the power to choose someone else.

- **Show respect.** Bring a notepad and take notes during the interview. This shows that you're interested and paying attention. Employers will reciprocate.

- **Test the waters.** Don't be shocked if an employer refuses to negotiate entry-level salaries. But after you've presented your value, do ask about the timing of performance reviews, as well as performance bonuses and how they're calculated. (Refer to Chapter 7 for salary talk.)

✔ **Storytell.** Prepare detailed true examples of all your skills, with as many examples from off campus as from on campus. But stay away from personal stories that may work on Facebook but are more personal than interviewers want to know.

✔ **Get insider secrets.** Graduate Careers Australia (graduatecareers.com.au) produces a range of graduate-related articles and research, covering industry and salary trends, employment opportunities and career development.

GradConnection (nz.gradconnection.com) is a free service that allows you to select the industry opportunities you're interested in hearing about. The site then emails you information about relevant opportunities as they arise.

Track down more resources to find out about interview questions by browsing for 'employer review websites'.

✔ **Be realistic.** Don't apologise for a lack of workplace experience beyond internships and student jobs. The employer already knows that you're starting out. Instead, explain how your experience at your part-time job waiting tables helped you hone your customer-service skills. This is a golden oldie but is especially important to young graduates.

Scripts for School Leavers and Graduates

You find suggested scripts for answering a large number of interviewing questions elsewhere in this book, especially in Chapters 14 through 19. In addition, the following script examples suggest strategies for smacking down bad press aimed specifically at recent graduates. Here goes:

✔ *You should hire me because I'm the best person for this job. Not only am I a hard worker and a fast learner, but I also bring a passion for excellence. I won't disappoint you. For example ___.*

✔ *Yes, I'm an experienced team player. I've had opportunities in my part-time jobs to work with a wide variety of people in age and background. I also work in teams during internships, and with university and sporting groups, to maximise my skills as a team player. On a recent project, for example, ___. I have also been fortunate to develop team leadership skills. I was captain of my soccer team for four years and was elected president of the Environmental Action Club at university. I enjoy making well-reasoned, well-thought-out decisions. For instance, when I ___.*

✔ *You asked how I handle conflict on a team. Basically, I try to make dispassionate judgements about what's best for the group and our goal, and then use good communication techniques to make my point. Let me tell you how I mediated a flap over ___.*

✔ *I am excited to learn that your company encourages volunteering for service work. I believe that people who give back to their community gain more than they give in terms of the experience as well as the skills developed. Based on my volunteer work with [name organisation], I find that service has added another dimension to my understanding of what people really want and how to meet those needs. I hope you'll select me for this position, because we're on the same page here.*

✔ *You asked me where I would like to be in five years. I would like to become the best marketing representative you have in the company. At the same time, I'll be preparing to take on greater responsibilities. For example, I've enrolled in an advanced-level marketing course online to be ready for future challenges. I love creative challenges, and I'm comfortable making decisions.*

✔ *You asked how well I work with people who are considerably older than me. That's great. In my work with the Cancer Council, which I've done for three years, all the volunteers have a mutual respect for each other and a great many are a decade or two older than I am. I look to older people to share their experience. I have also found they enjoy asking me to share what I know about new technologies and trends. So you could say it's a mutual admiration society.*

✔ *I have no problem working the hours you require. In fact, I would look forward to the opportunity to move around and see different areas of the company relatively early in my career, to get a better feel for what I can contribute down the line and where I want to go within the company. I'll work very hard to make a difference for this company and for the company's customers. I think my past managers and lecturers and tutors will back me up on that — would you like to see some of their letters of recommendation?*

✔ *Although I don't have formal work experience doing this exact kind of job, my vocational college education has given* me considerable background in this area. With a combination of my educational background and my job experience in the training, I know that I will be a productive new addition to your team, and I will go all out to make that happen.

✔ I know that many employers consider my generation to be somewhat difficult to manage and inspire. The joke I've heard is, 'You're in the Why generation — why aren't you more interested in your career prospects?' That's not me. I've been focused on joining a team such as this one all during the last year of my studies. And I've worked diligently to succeed at this goal, as I hope some of my earlier statements have conveyed. Do you think I'm the committed addition to your team whom you hope to hire?

Good Times and Your Future

The intergenerational shift in the workplace puts today's recent school and vocational college leavers and university graduates on the job market's red carpet. If that's you, enjoy your edge. Think about the following:

✔ Consider the flip-flop rhythm of the economy (did you study economics at school, by any chance?). Cyclical recessions and hiring slowdowns force younger as well as older people to stalk jobs for months on end.

Get ready for a competitive search

Prospects for new graduates move up and down depending on the economy. In recent years, many companies have cut back on the number of grads they're taking into their official programs. Even in the good times, employers receive many applications for each available starter-employee position. When you aren't snapped up by an on-campus recruiter, pull together a wish list of places you'd like to work and use online networking sites to connect with employees inside the prospective employer companies. Get more tips online from graduate and job search websites such as these:

✔ www.graduateopportunities.com

✔ www.careerone.com.au

✔ jobsearch.gov.au

✔ www.myfuture.edu.au

✔ nzunicareerhub.ac.nz

✔ As workforce ranks repopulate — until the year 2020 or so — with other young people who, like you, are techno savvy, you'll compete for jobs within your own age group.

✔ By far the biggest question mark for your future is how worldwide competition for the best jobs will affect Australians and New Zealanders of all ages. For example, outsourcing has removed a lot of entry-level roles. The economic misfortunes in the Northern Hemisphere in recent years have also seen young accountants and lawyers stay home in Australia or New Zealand, instead of create vacancies as they set off to work in the UK and Asia. And increasing levels of education mean a number of your job hunt competitors have a bachelor or an advanced degree just like you do.

As you gear up to begin your trip toward an award-winning work–life-balanced career, remember this one last tip: Some days you're the bug, some days you're the windshield.

Chapter 13

Star Turns for Prime-Timers

. . . .

In This Chapter

▶ Bringing age trouble out in the open

▶ Pushing back on age trouble

▶ Beating the overqualified turndown

▶ Sharing key tips to help highlight your experience as well as your attitude

. . . .

*I*f you'll never see your 20s and 30s again, you may have already run into an age obstacle that puts the brakes on your job hunt in a culture that values youth over experience.

But isn't age discrimination illegal? Of course it is. But does it happen? Sometimes or often, depending on your perspective.

Matt Bud leads The Financial Executives Networking Group (FENG), a 37,000-member US national organisation with local chapters. Most men and women who join FENG do so when they must find new jobs, but once employed, they tend to stay aboard and bond with other financial professionals as a kind of safety net against future joblessness.

Based on his vast experience, Bud observes that many employers have a profile of a winning candidate in mind. A rejection decision may not be discrimination: In the employer's eyes, the candidate simply may have the wrong profile for the job being filled.

So rather than refer to age bias, this chapter covers solutions to what I call *age trouble*, whether the trouble is due to discrimination or to a wrong profile. I help you recognise and overcome issues of age trouble when it stops you in your tracks, and provide some tips and scripts for highlighting your experience and positive attitude for interviewers.

Performing to Counter Age Prejudice

Age trouble shows up in many guises. In this overview, I present examples of questions that may mask common unspoken age-related concerns, followed by sample responses that show you don't have an expired shelf-life date stamped on your forehead.

Age and job performance

A big chunk of age trouble is centred on doubts that you can do the work. Here are three masked put-offs and push-backs:

✔ This is stressful and demanding work. How well do you work under pressure? (*Translation:* You may lack the stamina to do the job.)

I work well in all situations, especially when I'm under pressure. I like having deadlines. Early on, I learned to set internal deadlines for myself in all my projects, breaking the projects into segments so I always knew how I was doing. I consistently brought my projects in on time and on budget. Internal deadlines are my specialty.

✔ What do you do to maintain good health? (*Translation:* You don't look too healthy to me, and you may not be around long enough to justify training costs.)

Maintaining good health is a passion with me. My body mass index is similar to or better than that of most 30 year olds. I exercise several times a week. Once a week, I play cricket at my local club. And I watch what I eat.

✔ What office software do you use? Do you have a smartphone? Do you have a tablet? (*Translation:* You look like you do things the old-school way, and we're into new-school thinking.)

I'm proficient with [current business software]. I took a class for it on my own time last year at my local community college. My iPhone is with me 24/7. I make it a point to stay current with such major trends in our industry as [give one or two examples].

Age and money

In a world affected by business budgets, companies may see prime-timers as too pricey for value received, as the following two examples illustrate:

- ✔ What can you bring to this company? (*Translation:* You expect to earn more money to start than we want to pay; I can hire someone at half of what you want.)

  The contacts I have already made in my previous positions will help me be productive immediately, saving costs and earning revenues. I also bring a background that includes a related degree and successful years of experience in a similar position with another company. My background is an open book, showing that, by any measure, I represent great value!

- ✔ What are your monetary expectations of this job? (*Translation:* You're a seasoned worker accustomed to regular raises; our firm won't be able to make that kind of commitment, so why am I wasting time interviewing you?)

  Yes, I've been rewarded for my contributions to the bottom line for previous employers. Sometimes the compensation was in the form of a raise and sometimes it was a performance bonus for meeting goals. If you decide that I'm the right person for this position, I believe the monetary details won't present a problem, and I'll work with you on making that the case.

Age and attitude

Prime-timers may be perceived as living in another dimension of values and viewpoints or as set in their ways, as the following two questions and responses indicate:

- ✔ How would you go about doing this job? (*Translation:* You're accustomed to doing things your way, which may not be our way.)

  Although I've been quite successful in previous positions, I'm always happy to learn new and better ways to do things. Before suggesting any innovations, I would first make certain that I understand company policies and ways of working. I am very excited about this work opportunity and look forward to starting to work with you as soon as possible.

✔ You look as though you've led too accomplished a life to be returning to a career now. (*Translation:* You don't fit in with our young culture.)

I believe that my extensive experience in many productive settings will be of great benefit to your company because [give one or two examples]. I can work effectively with people of all ages. In fact, I really like working with young people because I respect their energy and vitality and fresh look at challenges.

Outing Elephants: Addressing Age Issues

Have you heard the expression 'If there's an elephant in the room, introduce it?' That's the topic of Chairman Matt Bud's advice to members of The Financial Executives Networking Group (FENG).

Bud warns FENG prime-timers that it's a huge mistake to avoid an age-related issue that the interviewer may be wary of bringing up directly. That's because an age zinger becomes an elephant in a small room — impossible to overlook, an obvious truth that is being ignored. Instead, get the sensitive question out in the open where you have a fighting chance to overcome the perception that you're too old for the job.

What follows is a part of what Bud counselled:

Among difficult questions an interviewer would like to ask you, a big one is age related: How much longer are you planning to work?

Close to being an illegal question even if the job is potentially long term or may involve a move, the interviewer may not ask, but the question is hanging out there, and until you get it out of the way, not much will happen during an interview.

If you choose not to address it, the interviewer may be trying to think up a way to politely ask you instead of listening to your very fine offerings about your many talents and how they could be applied to the job in question.

Don't wait to be put on the defensive; that may cause you to flush red-faced or stammer. My experience has been that most folks are uncomfortable with the answers to these kinds of questions and hope they won't come up. Wrong!

Get your story out in exactly the way you want it to be heard. When an elephant is in the room blocking the doorway to your progress, it is in the best interests of both parties to get this and other difficult questions out of the way early in the interview so that more important matters can be addressed.

The interview won't move forward until you expose and conquer hidden hiring objections.

Overcoming the Overqualified Label

Overqualified can be code for one of five perceptions. Interviewers may use the term to indicate that you

Radio babies and retirement reversal

Are you way over 50? If so, you may be in the generation born in the years 1930 to 1945, sometimes called radio babies (guess why) or traditionalists. Perhaps you decided to opt out of the workforce for a period of time and now want back in. How do you best answer the following question?

Why are you looking for a job after being retired for three years?

The effective answer is not that you need the money or that you were bored out of your mind with your job.

For a Show Stopper answer, follow this line of persuasion:

✔ Retired? Who retired? Explain that you didn't actually do the R-word. Discuss positive reasons for taking time off. Everyone needs to refresh and refill from time to time. Now you're opting back in.

✔ Discuss work with enthusiasm and declare that you're itching to get back to it.

✔ Describe how you can contribute to the company in chapter-and-verse detail.

✔ Have too many years' experience

✔ Have too much education

✔ Will want to be too highly paid

✔ Are too rigid with demands

✔ Are too rusted with obsolete skills

In my observation, when you're told you're overqualified for a position, you can usually chalk it up to the first perception: age trouble.

But Dallas-based Tony Beshara is a job-finding whiz who disagrees that being rated as overqualified for a position is because of age trouble, and he has strong credentials to back up his opinion. Beshara runs Babich and Associates, one of the US's most successful job-placement firms, and he personally has connected thousands of people with employment. Beshara says:

> *When a candidate of any age applies for a job one step or more below the level of his or her previous position, a hiring authority is going to be concerned that the candidate will be underemployed, depart as soon as something better turns up, and leave the authority holding the blame for a bad choice. The same overqualified tag could be applied to a 35 or 40 year old candidate, but since the predominant numbers of people going down the career ladder are in their 50s, the overqualified experience appears to be an age thing, but it's not.*

In either case, whether you're dealing with age trouble or not, why go down with the one-word punch of being rated as 'overqualified'? Come back with a strong response — or a pre-emptive strike to clear the air.

Try the following tactics when you hear the 'O' (overqualified) word:

✔ Clarify the interviewer's concerns. Find out whether the interviewer really thinks you're overqualified — or just over-aged — and whether you'll want to earn too much money or be bored by the position.

✔ Enthusiastically address the interviewer's concerns, emphasising the positive. Explain how you can grow in this position — today a clerk, tomorrow a back-up manager.

✔ Show how you can use your experience to benefit the company in solving long-term problems, building profit or assisting in other departments.

✔ Make sure that the interviewer understands your qualifications.

✔ In an office full of younger people, explain how you're an anchor: Experienced, calm, stable, reliable. You can provide continuity.

Here are six model responses to the overqualified put-off:

Overqualified? Some would say that I'm not overqualified, but fully qualified. With due respect, can you explain the problem with someone doing the job better than expected?

Fortunately, I've lived enough years to have developed the judgement that allows me to focus on the future. Before we speak of past years, past titles and past salaries, can we look at my strengths and abilities and how I've stayed on the cutting edge of my career field, including its technology?

I hope you're not concerned that hiring someone with my solid experience and competencies would look like age bias if, once on the job, you decided you'd made a mistake and I had to go. Can I present a creative idea? Why don't I work on a trial basis for a month? I realise there is a six-month [or three-month] probation but I am willing to work knowing it's just a one-month trial.

This job is so attractive to me that I'm willing to sign a contract committing to stay for a minimum of 12 months. There's no obligation on your part. How else can I convince you that I'm the best person for this position?

My family's grown. And I'm no longer concerned with title and salary — I like to keep busy. A reference check will show I do my work on time and do it well as a team member. I'm sure we can agree on a salary that fits your budget. When can we make my time your time?

Salary is not my top priority. Not that I have a trust fund, but I will work for less money, will take direction from managers of any age, will continue to stay current on technology, and will not leave you in the lurch if Hollywood calls to make me a star. And I don't insist that it's my way or the highway.

When the boss is your kid's age

Tony G., a reader of my newspaper column, wrote to me to say that, at age 60, he had just landed an excellent position with a start-up company after being interviewed by the 33-year-old company president, who, coincidentally, is the same age as his son. The other three employees are in their late 20s, as are Tony's daughters. Tony credits his success to his lack of *neophobia* (fear of new things).

'I think I was offered the job because of my attitude during the interview.

I made it clear to the young boss that I would rather work with people in 'your age bracket' because there is so much energy and new, fresh ideas. That's the environment where I want to work,' Tony said with conviction.

Advising other prime-timers, Tony added, 'Think young, think responsibly, and always be prepared to put something solid and attractive on the interview table.'

Mastering Top Tips for Prime-Timers

As good actors and actresses grow older, they no longer have to prove their talent, but they do have to prove that they still have what it takes to play a demanding role.

Take the following A-game hints to heart, two of which are suggested by contributing experts Liz Ryan, acclaimed speaker and writer on networking, and Tony Beshara, author of *Unbeatable Resumes* (AMACOM, 2011):

- ✔ Experiment with statements clarifying that contributing to the employer's goals is your first priority.

- ✔ Tell interesting true stories that illustrate your high energy, fresh enthusiasm and willingness to compete.

- ✔ Carry yourself with a young attitude. Enter the room with pep in your step.

- ✔ Liz Ryan advises that you think of concrete examples of times when you overcame an obstacle, made a save and had a breakthrough solution. Talk about how you deal with change. Work these things into the conversation before they're asked. Overcome any sense that people your age can't hustle.

✔ Tony Beshara suggests that you build rapport with an interviewer by mirroring his or her body language in the first few minutes. But as the interview develops, present yourself in an open, direct and assertive manner. Keep your feet planted on the floor, keep your arms open at your sides or on the arms of a chair, and lean forward just enough to make good eye contact. If your body language isn't appropriate, your words may never be heard.

✔ Don't enter an interviewing room with the attitude that your experience should speak for itself. Merely listing your tasks doesn't impress employers. Instead, answer the so-what question: Explain what difference you made and how your experience translates to their needs right now.

✔ Downplay ancient history. Unless you have a compelling reason to look way back in your career, focus your comments on the past 10 or 15 years. Talk only about your past experience that relates to the job at hand.

✔ To get around being seen as a tiresome know-it-all, don't constantly say 'I know'. Instead, acknowledge an interviewer's statement with 'That's interesting' or 'You make a good point' or 'I see what you mean'.

✔ Don't fall into the trap of thinking 'uppity child' when you're being interviewed by a younger hiring manager. Mutual respect is the right tone — even when the interviewer is young enough to be your kid.

✔ Use the question technique to avoid seeming to take charge of the interview: 'Did I fully explain how I can make a difference in solving the problem we've just discussed?' or 'Have I left unanswered any questions that you may have about my being the best person for this position?' When the answer indicates no reservations remain, smile and ask, 'When do I start?'

Keeping Your Career Fit

Everyone 50 and over knows that scooping up choice jobs isn't the cinch it often was when you were younger. As a prime-timer, you can greatly improve your odds of being chosen by learning new and improved job search skills, particularly the A-game interviewing techniques that determine what comes next in your life.

Part IV
Answering Questions with Confidence

Five Tips for Writing Your Personal Commercial

- ✔ **Avoid seeming stiff:** Add pauses, smiles, gestures and timing.

- ✔ **Describe your experience, competencies and skills:** Include the skills that are relevant to the type of position you want.

- ✔ **Make the information interesting:** Illustrate your sales pitch of your experience and skills with true stories. Storytell.

- ✔ ***Sell* rather than *tell*:** Let employers know what you've got and why they want it, rather than just providing the bare facts.

- ✔ **Practise your commercial:** First try your interview sales pitch out away from the spotlight of an interview — check out participation in a local chapter of Toastmasters International, for example.

Check out a free online article for tips on making the most of your education while interviewing at www.dummies.com/extras/successfuljobinterviewsau.

In this part . . .

✔ Provide interviewers with a better understanding of who you are and where you see yourself going, and sell yourself with your very own marketing pitch.

✔ Outline how much you know about the company you're interviewing for, and highlight your relevant skills and competencies.

✔ Remove the guesswork by clarifying how your experience is relevant and helpful in the context in which you're interviewing.

✔ Handle sticky questions and deal with any hard-to-market aspects of your special situation.

Chapter 14

Tell Me about Yourself

. . . .

In This Chapter

▶ Explaining away multiple online identities

▶ Separating strong from wrong answers about you

▶ Breaking a leg with a big-time branding brief

▶ Answering specific questions about you and your experience

. . . .

*Q*uestions and answers are dialogue on the stage of job interviews. This chapter illustrates response strategies that put you front and centre for selection when you're asked about the kind of person you are as related to the employer's bottom line.

Working from an employer's perspective, interviewers seek to discover what's right with you and what's wrong with you. Some interviewers are experts at making that call — others not so much.

In this chapter, I talk about how central this information is to a full understanding of how to sell yourself for any attractive job to any employer.

But First, Who Are You — Really?

Does your job search stretch across several industries, and maybe even more than one career field? If so, don't be surprised to wake up one day and be shocked to learn that your true identity is unclear — even suspect — to hiring authorities.

I'm talking not about the fearsome fraud of identity theft, but about multiple — and sometimes conflicting — online identities that can result from a broad digital job search.

The problem with multiple identities

Why is the issue of multiple online identities emerging as a dilemma for job seekers in this digital age? Why is it important to you? What can you do about it?

The answers to these questions become clearer after you review the underlying reasons a confused online identity has consequences in the job market. Here's a recap of those reasons, followed by examples:

- ✔ **Job history focus is a hiring magnet.** Employers try to minimise financial risk by hiring people who are doing, or who have recently done, the same job they're filling. Employers are less interested in taking a chance on you if you lack proven qualifications for the job.

- ✔ **Relevant industry experience is highly valued.** Even if you haven't done the exact job for which you're a candidate, are you at least in the same industry or a closely related one? Employers want to know that you've survived the bumps in their industry for a specified number of years — or, at least, that you understand the industry's behaviour in the marketplace.

- ✔ **A tailored resume is widely preferred.** Employers like you to customise your resume to show exactly how you're perfectly qualified for their job opening — not sort-of qualified, not maybe qualified and certainly not flat-out unqualified. By contrast, generic resumes and social media profiles usually miss the mark of spelling out that you provide the exact 'fit' for a specific job.

Examples of online multifaceted identities

Imagine this scenario: Suppose you have a genuine work history that includes these three main occupations and industries:

- ✔ Retail pharmacist
- ✔ Electronics manufacturing manager
- ✔ Replacement-window sales manager

You need a job, and you would work again in any of these three roles. That's why you blast three online versions of your resume and public profile all over the internet.

After awhile, you receive a call to interview for a job at a hospital pharmacy. Well, the nibble seems like good news, even though your last pharmacy gig was nine years ago, right? Not so fast. Once inside the interview room, sunny skies quickly turn cloudy.

The interviewer kicks off the meeting by asking which of your three resumes and profiles best describe your real expertise. Is it You 1? You 2? You 3? Are you a butcher, baker or candlestick maker?

Taken aback, you quickly realise the interviewer must have Googled you and discovered you seem to be three different people with three very different sets of qualifications.

Your prospects quickly go from bad to worse when the interviewer tartly says that the hospital pharmacy isn't planning to sell replacement windows or manufacture electronics, but does plan to hire a pharmacist with heavyweight experience in the retail pharmacy industry. 'So who are you, really?' the interviewer asks.

The rest of the discussion doesn't go well for you, not only because you've been away from the pharmacy industry for a number of years, but also because the interviewer's directness catches you off guard — and you certainly don't want to admit you're desperate to find employment in this decade of a shaky job market. Gulp!

The internet never forgets! To avoid your own episodes of this simmering-under-the surface dilemma, why not merely post differing 'private' versions of profiles and resumes? An obvious solution but, alas, not much remains hidden on the internet today.

Most hiring professionals now Google candidates and screen them on social media before inviting them to interview. In order, here's what they look for:

- ✔ Work history
- ✔ Education and training
- ✔ Recommendations from previous employers

> ✔ Hobbies and interests
>
> ✔ Activities and 'likes'
>
> ✔ Posted comments
>
> ✔ Group affiliations
>
> ✔ Pictures and videos
>
> ✔ Comments and links posted by candidate's friends

Although most of what employers look up online is pretty standard information, some recruiters try to uncover more controversial stuff using a new breed of social media screening and monitoring service, such as the PeopleCheck service based in New South Wales. Such a digital background-checking service can crack open even closed databases in the deep web.

For details of how easily your life and career path can become an open book, browse for articles online such as 'Data Mining: How Companies Now Know Everything About You,' by Joel Stein.

The multiple-identity pitfall is being noticed by experts who pay attention. As career-management legend John Lucht (www.ritesite.com) says, 'A good rule is to assume that everything you put out online will be read — *and in the context of everything else you have put out.*'

Career authority Miriam Salpeter (www.keppiecareers.com) comments that the dilemma of multiple online identities is certainly a modern job seeker's problem and makes this observation: 'Gone are the days of being able to have multiple job/career personalities in place without being found out! There is really no perfect answer, but there are some considerations.'

Salpeter, who is the author of the top-rated book *Social Networking for Career Success* (Learning Express), offers a number of ways to defuse the confused online identity problem before it happens, including this tip:

> *Don't post multiple versions of your resume all over the internet. In general, posting resumes online is not a useful strategy, anyway. If you're a job seeker with several targets, it's even less constructive to plaster information that may cause someone to think you can't decide what you want to do.*

Before digital days, positioning yourself as a perfectly qualified candidate for a specific job wasn't so steep a hill to climb as it is for some candidates today.

Answering a Very Broad Question about Yourself

In trying to figure out whether you're the right person to hire, interviewers usually start with the parent of self-revealing questions, often phrased as a statement: *Tell me a little about yourself.*

No matter how the question is worded, take care to get your act together for it, because it comes early in an interview — at the very time when an interviewer is forming an initial impression of you.

A good beginning sets the stage for the halo effect to kick in (refer to Chapter 8). The *halo effect* happens when an interviewer is impressed with you right off the bat and may assume that if you excel in one area, you excel in others.

 When you start to tell the interviewer about yourself, focus on aspects of your life that *illustrate your value as a candidate for the position you seek.* In addition to knowing that you have competencies, skills and experience related to the potential work, employers want to feel confident that you're the sort of person who

- ✔ Can do the job
- ✔ Will do the job
- ✔ Gets along with others while doing the job

Employers want to know how well you accept management direction. They want to know whether you have a history of slacking off as you get too comfortable on a job. They want to know whether — despite their lack of long-term commitment to you — you will jump ship at an inconvenient time if another employer dangles more money before your eyes.

When answering the Tell Me About Yourself question, bear the following thought in mind: *Focus on the Best You.*

A contrarian expert speaks

In the Different-Strokes-for-Different-Folks Department: Ace US placement professional Neil P McNulty (www.mcnultymanagement.com) has made hundreds of individual placements over 25 years. McNulty is a cut-to-the-chase kind of guy who advises his candidates to stick to business. Here's McNulty's take on the Tell Me About Yourself question:

Job hunting book experts say the question is asked because the interviewer wants to hear how you organise your thoughts, learn how you articulate your career ambitions and see how you present yourself when under pressure. That's not always the case.

The real reason it's asked is often because the interviewer is unprepared, doesn't know where to begin and, while you are speaking, he or she is trying to figure out what to ask you next.

I teach candidates to give a two-minute (max) chronological rundown of their professional history — no personal information — just a list of positions held, ending the rundown with this statement: This brings us to today. Tell me, what exactly do you want someone to do for you in this position? The tactic gives the interviewer a direction to go and also gives the candidate a 'needs target' to shoot at as the interview develops.

In sticking to the Best You theme, you may ask, 'But isn't that kind of like lying?' No. Lying is a time bomb that doesn't travel well.

I know a woman who did not inflate her previous salary — instead, she did the opposite, lowering it because she didn't want to be considered overqualified for a job she wanted. After 11 months, she was fired for lying when her reference checks finally caught up with her. The week before that, she had been offered a promotion!

Always be honest about the wonderful parts of you. But don't wildly exaggerate your best traits to the extent that your performance bears no relationship to your promise — remember that the piper who lives down the road will demand to be paid, and perhaps paid at a very inconvenient time.

Shade your answers to pack a punch

A careful questioner hears not only your lyrics, or content, in response to the self-defining question. The questioner also listens to your music and where you choose to turn up the volume:

- ✔ Do you focus on your competencies and skills, your education and training as they relate to the job? The interviewer is likely to conclude — *hooray!* — that you're work oriented.

- ✔ Do you focus on your hobbies? The interviewer may decide that you're more interested in your leisure hours, working only because you don't want to starve to death.

- ✔ Do you focus on your present job? The employer may think that you're still attached to your current haunts and not ready to move on. Or that you'll cynically use a job offer merely to leverage a counteroffer from your boss.

Narrow the question

You can jump right in and answer the Tell Me About Yourself question, or you can ask for prompts:

> *I can tell you about experience and accomplishments in this industry, or the education and training that qualify me for this position, or about my personal history. Where shall I start?*

Employers typically answer that they want to hear about both your work and relevant background — or a little bit of everything.

Writing Your Marketing Pitch

The sensible way to make star tracks in responding to a request to tell about yourself is to memorise — literally memorise — a personal commercial about yourself. Your 'show and sell' bit should run between one and two minutes.

Think for a few seconds about what a commercial does. It focuses on selling a product in a blink of time. It grabs your attention fast with information of interest to you. Then it tells why you should buy the product.

Your personal commercial works exactly the same way by enabling you to

- ✔ Grab employers' interest with a confident statement about yourself and your value related to the job you want
- ✔ Support that statement with specific facts
- ✔ Sell employers on why they should hire you instead of someone else

I wasn't kidding about memorising your personal commercial. Practise until it sounds natural. Just like an actor, you need to learn your script and deliver it in character. No stumbling. No ad-libbing.

Perhaps you're not so sure about my advice to memorise your script. Won't that make you sound as canned as a tin of tuna? Maybe. But which would you prefer — to sound a bit stiff or to flounder about as though you have no idea why you're there, why you're right for the job or why you have marbles in your mouth? Duh.

Depending on your experience level and the job you're trying to land, your personal commercial can include any or all of the following information:

- ✔ Academic degree
- ✔ Branding brief (see the sidebar 'New tool: The branding brief', at the end of this chapter)
- ✔ Competencies, skills and experience for the job
- ✔ Date of expected graduation (if applicable)
- ✔ General goals
- ✔ Honours or achievements
- ✔ Positions of leadership
- ✔ Specific job training

Raising the Curtain on Specific Questions about You

For the following questions in this chapter, *Show Stoppers* are answers that work for you; *Clunkers and Bloopers* are answers that work against you.

What is your most memorable accomplishment?

Show Stoppers

> ✔ Relate an accomplishment directly to the job for which you're interviewing.
>
> ✔ Give details about the accomplishment, as if you're telling a story.
>
> ✔ Describe the challenge, the action you took and the results (known as the CAR technique).

Clunkers and Bloopers

> ✔ Give a vague or unfocused answer.
>
> ✔ Discuss an accomplishment with no connection to the job you want.
>
> ✔ Discuss responsibilities instead of results.

Where do you see yourself five years from now? How does this position fit with your long-term career objectives?

Show Stoppers

> ✔ Say you hope your hard work has moved you appropriately forward on your career track.
>
> ✔ Answer realistically: In a changed business world where a long-term job may mean three years, speak of lifelong education to keep abreast of changes in your field and self-reliance for your own career.
>
> ✔ Describe short-term, achievable goals and discuss how they will help you reach your long-term goals.

✔ Explain how the position you're interviewing for will help you reach your goals.

✔ Strive to look ambitious, but not so much so that you threaten the hiring manager.

Clunkers and Bloopers

✔ Say that you want the interviewer's job.

✔ Describe unrealistic goals.

✔ Flippantly say that you expect to see yourself in mirrors and on YouTube.

✔ State goals the company doesn't need or can't satisfy.

What is your greatest strength?

Show Stoppers

✔ Anticipate and prepare to discuss up to five strengths, such as:

• Ability to learn quickly

• Cool, analytical temperament under pressure

• Leadership skills

• Proficiency at solving problems

• Skill in managing your work schedule

• Team-building skills

• Willingness to do extra work

✔ Discuss only strengths related to the position you want.

✔ Use specific examples to illustrate. Include statistics and testimonials.

Clunkers and Bloopers

✔ Discuss strengths unrelated to the job you want.

✔ Fumble around, saying that you don't feel comfortable bragging about yourself.

✔ Sell yourself too hard without delivering tangible evidence to back up your claims.

Expert contrarian discusses strengths

Placement pro Neil McNulty notes that placement experts advise you to have at least two or three significant achievements to describe, preferably in mini-story format.

'That is good information,' McNulty says. 'What they leave out is the fact that most of the entire job-hunting populace consists simply of average, hardworking, everyday people — most of whom have not done anything of tremendous importance. I teach such candidates that I place to answer this way:

I have done many things that I consider significant, but nothing that

really rocked the business world. The bottom line is that I am a hardworking, results-oriented, high-energy individual who gets the job done — and done right. My work is always on time, of correct quantity and quality and, if you hire me, you can expect nothing less, whatever the task.

My two cents: Rarely is a job search question so universal in outcome that any given rule must always be followed. Thanks, Neil McNulty, for another slant.

✔ Nominate a non-work achievement such as being president of the parents' body at your child's school (unless you're interviewing for a job selling school supplies). Discriminatory? Yes, but studies show that mums in particular can be wrongly seen as less committed to jobs than either childless women or men (with or without kids). As the number of stay-at-home dads is growing, time will tell if they'll start facing the same prejudice when returning to work.

What is your greatest weakness?

Show Stoppers

✔ Because of the corrective action you took, you were able to transform a starting point of failure into a success story of strength. Four examples follow:

• *Not being a natural techie, I was underperforming when I first worked with [X] using a range of software needed for the job. So I attended a course in my own time and now I'm the best administrative assistant in my office.*

• *I didn't always know what I was doing — right or wrong — when I took my first managerial position. So I took online* classes in managerial techniques, read management books and paid attention to how managers whom I admired operated. As a result, I give careful thought to the quality of guidance that I give my direct reports before launching a project. I can always improve but my track record shows my leadership worked to improve the productivity and achievements of my teams.

- *I've had trouble remembering the timing of every appointment when I had to move like lightning across town from one sales call to another sales call. But I've corrected that scheduling problem with this terrific smartphone app. I haven't missed an appointment since I got it.*

- *I'm determined to complete whatever I start, and occasionally I can see myself getting too attached to the goal. To counter this, I've developed a habit of taking a step back to evaluate the value of completing a project to the original plan and making a course correction to better serve the needs of the business. Shall I tell you about the time when I ___?*

✔ Cite a shortcoming you're working on, even if you haven't completely turned the weakness around — yet. Three examples follow:

- *I'm working on my time-management skills, quickly learning not to take on an overload of work if it threatens the quality of my work products. For example, I now write to-do lists and assign priorities.*

- *I'm working on cooling my tendency to be impatient. It's my nature to want to accomplish things as fast and efficiently as possible, and when others stall my progress, I lose patience. I remind myself every morning that others are busy people too. Now I cut co-workers more slack on getting back to me before I send a friendly reminder.*

- *English is my second language. But I'm taking a class and listening to everyday conversational speech on TV, and my language ability is getting better every day.*

✔ Balance a weakness with a compensating strength. Three examples follow:

- *I'm not a global thinker. But being detail minded, I'm a top-notch staffer to an executive who is a big-picture person.*

- *As a newcomer to this city, I can't bring a clientele to this job, but I can use my talent for public presentations to build one faster than you can say 'Give me a quote'. I have a plan to attract clients by quickly becoming known as a speaker at local club meetings and civic events.*

Wacky weakness

Samuel Goldwyn spent much of his legendary life as chief of Metro-Goldwyn-Mayer, a major movie studio. He was widely known as 'Mr Malaprop' for making an amusing series of misstatements that defied the English language. When a reporter asked a young Samuel Goldwyn if he'd ever made a picture, the film executive's answer was charming:

Yes, but that's our strongest weak point.

- *I have not held a job with the title 'project manager' but as you can see from my career history, I have managed major and detailed projects in my past three roles.*

✔ Choose a weakness that doesn't matter to the job's success. An example follows:

- *I'm a very organised person, but you'd never know it by looking at my desk, which sometimes qualifies for the cover of* Better Landfills *magazine.*

✔ Rhetorically rephrase the question aloud to make your shortcoming seem less of a minus. One example follows:

- *Let me think ... what attributes, when improved, would make me perform even better in this job? Hmm ...*

✔ Then identify areas in which you want more training or guidance.

Clunkers and Bloopers

✔ Mention a brutally honest negative, such as you're hard to work with, you're easily bored, you're lazy, you don't get along well with co-workers from different backgrounds, you have a poor memory or a hot temper, or you're exhausted by stress.

✔ Fall back on clichés. Examples: You're a workaholic. *(My boss has to shove me out the door every night to make me go home.)* You're a perfectionist. *(The devil is in the time-eating details, and I sweat every one.)* Or cutesy answers such as 'chocolate' or 'shoes' to questions about your greatest weakness.

✔ Say you have no weaknesses.

✔ Volunteer key weaknesses that were likely to go unnoticed in the hiring decision.

Would you rather work with others or alone? How about teams?

Show Stoppers

✔ Discuss your adaptability and flexibility in working with others as a leader or a follower. At heart, you're always a team player but, in certain situations, you prefer to work alone.

✔ Give concrete examples.

✔ Mention the importance of every team member's contribution.

Clunkers and Bloopers

✔ Appear to be overly dependent on a team to see you through.

✔ Let the interviewer think that you're a pushover, willing to carry the load of team members who don't contribute.

✔ Say you don't like to work with teams.

What is your definition of success? Of failure?

Show Stoppers

✔ Show that your success is balanced between your professional and personal lives.

✔ Relate success to the position you want.

✔ If you have to talk about failure, do so positively. Show how you turned a failure into a success, or discuss how and what you learned from the failure.

✔ Demonstrate that you're a happy person who thinks the world is more good than bad.

Clunkers and Bloopers

✔ Spend a great deal of time talking about failure.

✔ Say that you've never failed or made mistakes.

✔ Discuss success as a ruthless, take-no-prisoners shot to the top.

How do you handle stressful situations?

Show Stoppers

- ✔ Give examples of how you've dealt with job stress.
- ✔ Discuss what you do to relax, refresh and refill.
- ✔ Give positive illustrations of how job stress makes you work harder or more efficiently.

Clunkers and Bloopers

- ✔ Say that you avoid stress. (What me, worry?)
- ✔ Imply that stress is usually the result of lack of preparation or knowledge.

Is there anything else I should know about you?

Show Stoppers

- ✔ Discuss any selling points the interview failed to uncover and relate those selling points to the job you want.
- ✔ Repeat the selling points you've already discussed and remind the interviewer why you're the best candidate for the job.

Clunkers and Bloopers

- ✔ Say 'No.' And not another word.
- ✔ Remark that you will require the first two weeks off every February because that's when your family always holidays.

Why should I hire you?

Show Stoppers

- ✔ Prepare at least three key reasons to roll off your tongue that show how you're better than the other candidates.
- ✔ Use specific examples to illustrate your reasons. *(My managers have consistently described me as easy to manage. I can apply the same dedication here that won me employee awards elsewhere. I believe I could really contribute in this role, and I hope I have given you reasons to believe that too. Are there any areas you'd like me to discuss further?)*

✔ Share something unusual or unique about you that will make the interviewer remember you. You can refer to a branding brief, described in the sidebar at the end of this chapter; leave a print copy behind.

Clunkers and Bloopers

✔ Dance around this question (*I live nearby*) without really addressing it.

✔ You would be an asset to the company footy tipping contest; you're tired of living with your parents; your mortgage payment is overdue; your brother needs help paying off his student debt; you need a change of scenery.

✔ Tell the interviewer, 'You need to fill the job.'

Mastering More to Tell about Yourself

Most of us have scant experience in interviewing for jobs. Contrast that with the experience of hiring authorities who interview for a living. Some human resource specialists and even hiring managers ask tricky questions that are spin-offs of 'Tell me about yourself'.

New tool: The branding brief

Kathryn Kraemer Troutman, executive career consultant and CEO of The Resume Place, Inc. (www.resume-place.com) recommends that job seekers devise an abbreviated personal marketing message, one that she terms a *branding brief*. The length of a branding brief is 20 to 30 seconds, or about 100 words.

A similar synopsis may also be called a *mini-elevator speech*, a *personal branding message* or a *career profile summary*; all these terms refer to a capsule of your 'story' as it relates to an employer. All are shorter than your personal commercial, which I describe earlier in this chapter.

Consider incorporating a branding brief within your one- to two-minute personal commercial for interviews, using it as a standalone statement in networking or leaving it behind after a job interview. A branding brief has more 'sell' than a factual short bio and is presented in a less formal style.

A branding brief headlines what you are known for. It identifies your special characteristics and achievements of interest to an employer. You can use a branding brief to help people remember who you are, why you're memorable and when they should seek you. Troutman explains:

In constructing a branding brief, describe your top characteristics and how they can contribute to the mission of an organisation that you hope to join. Clearly state how you can help achieve the organisation's mission.

Here are a few of Troutman's branding brief content examples:

✔ My name is Keri Bright, and I formerly taught English at Martingale High School, where I was known for establishing community literacy programs to teach immigrants how to read and write English. My bilingual skills would be useful as an aide in the member of parliament's office.

✔ I successfully worked as a library technician in the James River Library, with diverse accomplishments ranging from multimedia productions and program development, to speaker recruitment and publication selection for special markets.

✔ After getting real library experience for six years, I invested in an information and library studies degree program to upgrade my professional competencies and skills. Now I'm ready to begin work on blending technology, archives and library services in efficient and affordable programs to excite library patrons.

✔ My career as a logistics specialist — some people call that supply-chain specialist — is very rewarding as I work to see that important materials and resources get to the right place at the right time for the right price. I'm a perfect fit for your position, where I would continue working my magic for your customers — managing inventory, distributing goods, and monitoring the quality of materials provided.

Chapter 15

What Do You Know about This Job and Our Company?

In This Chapter

▶ Proving that you understand the job, the company and the industry

▶ Answering sample questions for practice

*W*hen you're aiming for a professional or managerial job, expect a number of questions to be fired at you to test your knowledge of the position, company and industry.

Even when your aspirations are less lofty and your goal is to be hired as a supporting player, understanding the topics in this chapter can put you in the take-a-bow category of candidates.

Understanding the Job, Company, Industry — and How They All Fit Together

Employers expect you to grasp what the job entails and how it fits into the overall company picture. They're even more impressed if you've looked into what the company does and where it stands in its industry.

An interviewer may test your knowledge for a managerial or more senior job with questions like this:

> *Where would you rank this company in the marketplace and why?*

Such a question requires you to go into some detail about the company's place in the scheme of things — its products, profitability, industry position, goals and vulnerability to buyout.

An interviewer may not look at your answers for definitive details, but he is interested in how you arrived at your conclusions. You could say:

> *You ranked second in the industry in total earnings last year, so that's a positive. Your level of debt is a little high, but that was the result of tooling up for your next line of products due out in June. If the new line is as successful as forecast, most of the rest of the company debt will be wiped out by new sales, leaving the company with a shot at being the most financially secure in the industry. Plus, you still enjoy an enormous potential for growth in the near future.*

If you mention problems in the company's performance, offer general solutions (additional training, financial fixes, workforce restructuring and the like). Otherwise, you appear clueless or, as some interviewers may say, *Nice cage, no bird.* Or, *all foam, no beer.* Or, *all hat, no cattle.* You get the idea.

To model credibility, you can beef up your general solutions with specifics that suggest you're doing more than merely guessing. That is, cite statistics and figures to back up the problems you note, along with your bright ideas to remedy them.

A caution: Reflect before following interviewing advice you may have read elsewhere that urges you to Superman-leap tall problems in a single bound. Certain difficulties may have eluded resolution by company managers for good reasons. On the outside looking in, chances are, you don't have all the facts on the ground.

The Questions

Look at the following questions and the strategies you can use to answer them as you gear up to show perfect casting with the job, and the company.

Choose strategies marked as *Show Stoppers*; avoid those indicated to be *Clunkers and Bloopers*.

What do you know about this position?

Show Stoppers

- ✔ From your research, discuss how the position fits into the company structure and how you would fit like a glove into that position.
- ✔ Mention how you can help the company achieve its goals.
- ✔ Confirm your understanding of the broad responsibilities of the position. Ask whether you missed any key points (thereby setting up topics to discuss your qualifications).

Clunkers and Bloopers

- ✔ Ask what the company makes.
- ✔ Use out-of-date data.

What do you know about our competition?

Show Stoppers

- ✔ Discuss the current climate of the industry and how competitors are affected.
- ✔ Add details that show you truly understand the industry and the competition.
- ✔ Analyse the impact global competition is having on the industry.

Clunkers and Bloopers

- ✔ Say you know very little about the competition.
- ✔ Admit you recently interviewed with the competition.
- ✔ Reveal trade secrets from your current employer.

What are your opinions about some of the challenges facing our company?

Show Stoppers

> ✔ Show the depth of your research by discussing some of the company's upcoming projects.
>
> ✔ Mention several possible solutions to potential problems the company may be facing, acknowledging that you lack certainty without proprietary facts.

Clunkers and Bloopers

> ✔ Say you don't know of any challenges, but you're all ears.
>
> ✔ Mention problems but add no possible solutions.

What do you see as the direction of this company?

Show Stoppers

> ✔ Give a brief but somewhat detailed answer, displaying a solid grasp of the company's movement in the industry. Add how you can help.
>
> ✔ Support your answer with facts and figures, citing their sources.

Clunkers and Bloopers

> ✔ Make guesses because you haven't a clue.
>
> ✔ Offer no data to back up your comments.

Why did you apply to this company?

Show Stoppers

> ✔ Say that the position is a compelling opportunity and the company is a place where your qualifications can make a difference. Explain why.
>
> ✔ Relate that you heard about a new service the company is launching, which is somewhat related to a project you helped create in a previous job role or in your final year at university; say you find the potential exciting. Ask if the interviewer would like to hear about your project.

Clunkers and Bloopers

> ✔ Say the company is in an industry you've always wanted to try.
>
> ✔ Say you've always wanted to live in [location of the job].

Our company has a mission statement; do you have a personal mission statement — or personal vision?

Show Stoppers

> ✔ In one or two sentences, give examples of your values (customer service, ethics, honour, importance of keeping one's word and so on) that are compatible with the company's.
>
> ✔ Review the company's mission statement on its website and describe a compatible aim.

Clunkers and Bloopers

> ✔ Ask what a mission statement is.
>
> ✔ Ask for clarification on the meaning of values.

How will you help our company?

Show Stoppers

> ✔ Summarise how your key skills can help the company move toward its goals.
>
> ✔ Describe the wide circle of contacts and other intangible benefits you can bring to the company.

Clunkers and Bloopers

> ✔ Give a short answer with no specifics.
>
> ✔ Say you'll have to get back to the interviewer on that one.

Chapter 16

What Are Your Skills and Competencies?

In This Chapter

▶ Navigating competency-based interviews

▶ Spotting skills questions

▶ Addressing skills and competencies questions

▶ Practising with sample questions

*W*ith job security in today's market going the way of the ozone layer, the operative words are *skills* (what you can do) and, increasingly, a newer and broader employment concept termed *competencies* (how well you do what you do using natural talents). Competencies reflect characteristics, such as motivation, industriousness and attitudes.

This chapter walks you through preparing for skills- and competency-based questions, and how to answer them in the interview situation in a way that makes you shine.

Taking the Competency-Based Interviewing Approach

The *competency-based interviewing approach* attempts to look at the whole package where you're concerned. Suppose, for example, that you're a certified expert in Java and no question exists about your skill level. Competency questions attempt to uncover whether you also have the soft skills you need to pursue successful work projects where cooperation, communication and being organised are essential. (Or whether your prickly personality drives colleagues to the aspirin bottle.)

Competency-based models fall into two categories:

✔ *Work-based competencies* describe job-specific characteristics, skills and abilities, such as fluency in the English language or the ability to read topographical maps.

✔ *Behaviour-based competencies* describe all the other personal stuff you need, in addition to technical skills, to do the job well. Competencies include abilities like:

  • Adapting to new technologies

  • Keeping technical skills up-to-date

  • Planning for additional resources

  • Prioritising and planning work

  • Using time efficiently

A *competency-based interview* is highly structured and based on the premise that past success is the best predictor of future success. Many questions designed to reveal behavioural competencies begin with 'Tell me about a time when...' (Refer to Chapter 4 to find out about the behaviour-based interview.)

You can expect competency-based interviewing at larger companies and government departments and agencies. By contrast, small and medium-size employers (where most of the jobs are) tend to stick to skills discovery in their interview questions. Their interviewers make informal judgements about how well candidates will use their skills on the job.

Be aware that some overlap in everyday usage of terminology occurs: That is, one interviewer's *skills* is another interviewer's *competencies*. To keep it simple, in this chapter, I use the s-word — *skills*.

Recognising Skills Questions

Accomplishments, like some wines, don't always travel well. You catch an employer's eye with accomplishments, but when you change jobs, you leave your accomplishments behind. What you do pack along with you are the skills that enabled you to achieve those accomplishments: Mastering the subject, meeting deadlines and researching online, for instance. These skills are also referred to as 'transferable'.

Experienced interviewers move past the citations of what you did to discover how you did it — the essence of your skills.

Interviewers may be straightforward in trying to determine your skills through questions about specific work experiences:

> *Tell me about a time a supervisor gave you a new project when you were racing the clock to complete an earlier-assigned project.*

Or you may be tossed a pretend workplace scenario and asked how you'd handle the situation:

> *You're monitoring and integrating control feedback in a petrochemical processing facility to maintain production flow when the system suddenly goes down; what do you do?*

Other questions are less direct, going in a conversational side door to see how you react using such skills as conflict management and interpersonal relationships:

> *How would you deal with a difficult boss?*

To pull off a Show Stopper interview, learn to recognise questions that spotlight the skills you bring to a job stage.

Answering Questions about Your Skills

Use storytelling (refer to Chapter 4) to comprehensively answer skills questions. Remember, too, that social, or soft, skills (people skills) play a significant role in determining the winning candidate. Take pains to convince the interviewer that you're a pleasant individual who gets along with people.

Consider the question in the previous section about how you'd deal with a difficult boss. Here's an answer, underscored with storytelling that makes you look like a reasonable and conscientious person:

> *I would first try to make sure that the difficulty isn't walking around in my shoes. Then I'd read a few books on how to interact with difficult people. I've never*

had a boss I didn't like, but I have had to use tact on occasion.

On my last job, my boss and I didn't see eye to eye on the best software for an office application. I researched the issue in detail and wrote a short, fact-filled report for my boss. Based on this new information, my boss then bought the software I recommended.

This answer centres on research skills but also highlights patience and acceptance of supervision.

The Questions

The sample skills questions in this chapter are generalised for wider application, although, in an interview, you should expect skills questions that relate to your career field: *What computer skills do you have? Why do you think your technical skills are a match for this job? When is the best time to close a sale? What was your most difficult auditing problem and how did you solve it? Tell me about your typical workday as a probation officer.*

Note that questions in this chapter may seem to be close relatives of the questions in Chapter 17. The difference is that those in Chapter 17 are intended to draw out your qualities as a human being; the questions in this chapter go after your skills. Is it a big goof if you mix them up? Not at all. Both are reminders to keep your self-marketing pitch up and running.

What is the toughest job problem you've ever faced?

Show Stoppers

> ✔ Recall a problem, the *skills used in your action* to deal with it, and the successful results; this is a skills-detailed version of PAR (problem, action, result).

> ✔ Explain how you can apply those same skills to the prospective job.

Clunkers and Bloopers

> ✔ Recall a problem but not an accomplishment or skill related to it.

> ✔ Say you've searched your memory and can't recall a problem you couldn't handle.

What do you like least about gathering information to deal with a problem (research)?

Show Stoppers

✔ Comment that, wanting to do a first-rate job, you're uncomfortable when you're uncertain that you've compiled enough research to quit and make a decision that affects the wellbeing of others.

✔ Reveal that you enjoy solving problems but become impatient with repetitive answers leading to dead ends.

✔ Explain that you use multiple resources — websites, books, journals and expert people — and you become frustrated when key resources aren't adequate.

Clunkers and Bloopers

✔ Dismiss researching as work for the scholars among us, and say you prefer to be an action hero. (Even bank robbers have to case the job.)

✔ Admit you prefer outdoor work and aren't sure why you're here.

How good are you at making oral presentations?

Show Stoppers

✔ Discuss how you prepare. Name presentation skills. Mention specific instances when you've given a good show.

✔ Offer to give a one-minute oral presentation on a topic you've practised.

Clunkers and Bloopers

✔ Say that you never do them because you're terrified of speaking in front of large crowds.

✔ Admit you were roundly booed at your last political protest speech.

How would you rate your writing skills in comparison to your verbal skills?

Show Stoppers

✔ Discuss how both skills — as well as listening — are important to being a good communicator, and that while one or the other may be your strong suit, you're working to become strongly proficient at both speaking and writing. Explain how you're doing so — class work, independent study, membership in Toastmasters International or a writing group; show brief writing samples.

✔ Concretely explain a real communication situation in your past; describe how you communicated the information and the result.

✔ If you're a weak communicator, give a compensatory response that substitutes another skill for writing or verbal skills; for example, in a technical call centre, problem solving outweighs the need for golden tonsils and laudable business writing.

Clunkers and Bloopers

✔ Rate your skill in one area as better than the other and clam up.

✔ Say that public speaking gives you sweaty palms and you don't like it.

How do you deal with unexpected events on the job?

Show Stoppers

✔ Discuss how you immediately reprioritise your assignments in emergencies.

✔ Mention specific instances when you were able to complete a project (or projects) on time despite unforeseen complications.

Clunkers and Bloopers

✔ Tell how you just keep doing what you are doing until you're finished.

✔ Discuss an instance when an unexpected event resulted in disaster.

How do you organise your time?

Show Stoppers

🗸 Affirm that you put first things first. Each day you identify A-level tasks and get those done before moving on to B-level tasks. You return voicemail messages once or twice daily and urgent messages immediately.

🗸 Comment that you use up-to-date planning products. Name any planning software or apps you use as well as handheld devices, such as a Samsung Galaxy. These kinds of mentions show that you are techno-current. If you organise yourself on paper, mention a formal business product such as a Franklin Planner. (Pulling out a pocket calendar is like pulling out a slide rule.) Conclude with true examples showing that you've completed multiple tasks on time.

🗸 Discuss how you went through a typical day on one of your previous jobs.

Clunkers and Bloopers

🗸 Say that you don't usually handle more than one task at a time.

🗸 Reply that you don't wear a watch.

How do you delegate responsibility?

Show Stoppers

🗸 Discuss how you involve everyone in the overall picture.

🗸 Discuss specific projects that were successful because of your team effort.

Clunkers and Bloopers

🗸 Reveal that you like process detail; admit your micromanaging tendency to tell direct reports how to connect every dot.

🗸 Mention your belief that a task will be done right only if you do it yourself.

What's your experience with group projects (teamwork)?

Show Stoppers

- ✔ Mention a specific project, including the group goals and your particular responsibilities.

- ✔ Discuss your positive relationship with the project supervisor; compliment co-workers.

Clunkers and Bloopers

- ✔ Don't identify your responsibilities; just say you all worked together.

- ✔ Rip your co-workers as laggards and say you're sick of doing most of the heavy lifting without credit.

Why should I hire you?

Show Stoppers

- ✔ Summarise point by point why your qualifications match the employer's needs to a tee, adding any additional competitive edge you can honestly claim. (Rehearse in advance to avoid stumbles.)

- ✔ Include accomplishments and the skills that facilitated those accomplishments, plus relevant experience and training.

Clunkers and Bloopers

- ✔ Fail to make the 'perfect match' connection.

- ✔ Offer only clichés, such as 'I'm honest, hardworking and a fast learner', without factual backup illustrations.

Chapter 17

How Does Your Experience Help Us?

*I*n your working life, it's not your time as an employee that matters, but what you have done with that time. You can have ten years of skill-building experience — or you can have one year's experience with nine years of reruns. Solid experience is yet one more confirmation of your ability to do a top-notch job.

In this chapter, I cover ways you can highlight your experience to your advantage.

Making Your Experience Relevant

Psychologists insist that past behaviour predicts future behaviour. True or not, interviewers look at your yesterdays for clues on how well you'll perform in your tomorrows.

 Simply reciting your experience isn't going to excite an employer. You have to make the connection between then and now. You have to show exactly how your experience-based accomplishments make you the perfect candidate for the job opening.

When you're technically great but quiet and shy

Some people, including those who have exceptional technical talents, are sometimes very shy during interviews and appear to be introverted and timid. Is that you?

Here's a trick around that problem from Martin Yate, author of *Knock 'em Dead: The Ultimate Job Search Guide* (Adams Media Corporation, 2012) and a raft of other best-selling job search books. Yate says that if you reach across the desk to hand the interviewer papers, graphs and reports from your portfolio of work samples, the interviewer will ask you questions about the samples. Your answers will keep the flow of conversation going — and you'll answer the questions and won't come across as, well, bashful.

Whether you have a lot or a little experience, employers want to hire people who will continue to learn and grow to the benefit of their company. So as you answer the experience questions, focus not only on your experience, but also on how your efforts served the changing needs of your previous employer.

When you can show how you've successfully adapted in the past, convincing employers that you have what it takes to adapt your experience to their workplaces is easier.

After the interviewing Q&A begins, what should you do if you don't understand one of the questions? Don't be afraid to ask for clarification — *I'm not sure I understand your question, and I don't want to give you an irrelevant or incorrect answer.*

Answering the Questions

Questions that you may be asked about your work experience, along with suggested answering techniques (*Show Stoppers*) and definite mistakes (*Clunkers and Bloopers*), include the following:

What kind of experience do you have for this job?

Show Stoppers

✔ Gather information before answering. Ask what projects you would be working on in the first six months. Relate your experience to those projects, detailing exactly how you would go about working on them.

✔ Give specific examples of your success in dealing with similar projects in the past, focusing on results.

✔ Show how crossover (also known as transferable) skills drawn from even seemingly unrelated experience — such as waiting tables or planning events — apply to this project.

Clunkers and Bloopers

✔ Say you have no experience. Next question!

✔ Show that your experience overreaches this particular job — unless you know your overqualification is a plus or when your real agenda is to angle for a higher-level position.

In what ways has your job status changed since you got into this field?

Show Stoppers

✔ Mention that you've worked in X number of positions — from small to larger employers — with increasing responsibility; this position is a logical next level in your upward track record.

✔ Sketch advances in your line of work over the years. Describe how you've continued your education and training.

✔ Draw out hiring objections: Ask whether you failed to cover any key responsibilities. If there's a gap, show how you've handled missing responsibilities, perhaps in earlier positions.

Clunkers and Bloopers

✔ Omit mentioning key functions in your move upward. You'll look like you may need to catch up.

✔ Confirm that you've held the same job for ten years, with little change.

How long would it take you to make a contribution to our company?

Show Stoppers

> ✔ Explain how selecting you will shorten training time because your experience qualifies you as a turnkey candidate. You don't need to be brought up to speed. Name past challenges, actions and results.

> ✔ Estimate how long it would realistically take you to begin producing first-class work on a particular project. Then detail how you would go about working on the project. Forecast how much time you expect each step would take, being realistic but optimistic.

Clunkers and Bloopers

> ✔ Say you'll hit the ground running and smile.

> ✔ Say you can't become productive for at least four months (unless you're headed for an incredibly complex job in which a settling-in period lasting beyond three months is normal).

What are your qualifications?

Show Stoppers

> ✔ Item by item, connect your close fit between the job's requirements and your qualifications.

> ✔ Ask what specific projects or problems you may be expected to deal with and which have the highest priority.

> ✔ Identify the projects you've accomplished in the past that qualify you to work successfully on the projects the interviewer mentions.

Clunkers and Bloopers

> ✔ Assume you know what the interviewer wants to hear about and plunge in.

> ✔ When you have limited work experience, speak only of your education without weaving in nuggets of experience in your school lab work, volunteer work or student jobs.

How did you resolve a tense situation with a co-worker? Have you ever had to fire someone?

Show Stoppers

- ✔ First, discuss your analytical process for solving routine workplace problems (as advocated in conflict-resolution guidebooks). Storytell a specific example of a problem you solved.

- ✔ In a termination example, state the steps you took to help the fired person improve and save his job before making a termination decision.

- ✔ Emphasise that you follow company policy and that you're fair and tactful.

Clunkers and Bloopers

- ✔ Complain that colleagues unfairly ganged up on you.

- ✔ Discuss an example of when you fired someone because you just didn't like the person.

- ✔ Focus on how horrible the problem or employee was, naming names.

Give a specific example of teamwork when you had to put your needs aside to help a co-worker.

Show Stoppers

- ✔ Mention the importance of co-workers being able to rely on each other. Give a specific example, showing how you helped and that the reliance wasn't one-sided.

- ✔ Explain in the example that, although you went the extra mile for the team, your efforts did not cause you to skimp on your own duties. Perhaps you put in that extra effort on your own time.

Clunkers and Bloopers

- ✔ Comment that you're a team player and leave it at that.

- ✔ Say you can't recall any examples.

What did you like best at your last job?

Show Stoppers

> ✔ Help the interviewer to see a match from past to future by mentioning specific work experiences you were good at and enjoyed that are likely to be present in the prospective position.
>
> ✔ Speak about opportunities to plan your own day or to think outside the box.
>
> ✔ Confirm that you enjoyed being visible in a high-stakes effort, knowing that your work directly contributed to the company's bottom line.

Clunkers and Bloopers

> ✔ Blast your ex-job as a loser and say that's why you're here.
>
> ✔ Explain that nothing stands out as having been especially rewarding.

Describe a time that you had to work without direct supervision. Have you ever had to make department decisions when your supervisor was not available?

Show Stoppers

> ✔ Discuss your level-headed decision-making process. You don't rattle easily.
>
> ✔ Show that you're self-directed and self-motivated, but are happily willing to follow others' directions or to ask for assistance when needed.
>
> ✔ Storytell: Discuss a specific example of a time you had to make a decision without supervision. Choose an instance when you anticipated company needs and finished a project ahead of time or made a beneficial decision.

Clunkers and Bloopers

> ✔ Whine about being forced into a decision that turned sour.
>
> ✔ Admit that you've never worked without someone looking over your shoulder or telling you what to do.

Have you ever misjudged something? How could you have prevented the mistake?

Show Stoppers

> ✔ Briefly discuss a specific — but minor — example of misjudgement. Say what the mistake taught you and how it led you to improve your system for making decisions or solving problems.

> ✔ After talking about your example and what you learned from it, ask a question to refocus the discussion on your accomplishments — *Would you like to hear about a notable win as well as that loss?*

Clunkers and Bloopers

> ✔ Discuss a mistake that cost your employer plenty of time and money.

> ✔ Pass the blame to someone else.

> ✔ Say you've never misjudged anything.

Has a supervisor ever challenged one of your decisions? How did you respond?

Show Stoppers

> ✔ Identify an example of being challenged when you listened politely but supported your decision with research or analytical data, and you won over your critical supervisor.

> ✔ Add that even though you justified your decision, you were open to suggestions and comments. You're confident in your abilities but not closed minded or foolishly stubborn.

Clunkers and Bloopers

> ✔ Castigate your supervisor for trying to micromanage.

> ✔ Insist that you were right even though management reversed your decision.

In your current position, what are your three most important accomplishments?

Show Stoppers

> ✔ Mention six of your best work accomplishment stories. Ask which ones the interviewer would like to hear more about.
>
> ✔ After describing the top three, comment that you can expand the list. Consider having a sheet ready detailing specific accomplishments but couched in terms of how you could add value if given the role. You could also provide contact information for those who worked with you at those times. A move like this will work best in high-performing work cultures so do your homework on the employer organisation first.

Clunkers and Bloopers

> ✔ Laughingly remark that you have so many accomplishments that it's hard to choose just three.
>
> ✔ Admit that you're not sure what counts as an accomplishment.

Your experience doesn't exactly match our needs right now, does it?

Show Stoppers

> ✔ Don't agree. Instead, state that you see your fit with the job through a rosier lens. Your skills are cross-functional. Focus on how you can easily transfer your experience in related areas to learning this new job.
>
> ✔ Stress that you're dedicated to learning the new job quickly. Give two true examples of how you learned a job skill much faster than usual.
>
> ✔ Say you don't have any bad habits to unlearn and discuss your good work habits that will help you get the job done efficiently and well.

Clunkers and Bloopers

> ✔ Agree, smile and say nothing to compensate for the mismatch — unless, of course, you don't want the job.
>
> ✔ Let the door hit you on the way out.

Chapter 18

Talking about Your Special Situation

. . . .

In This Chapter

▶ Overcoming hidden issues on the hiring road

▶ Handling the discussion when you've been fired, demoted, spent time in prison or have gaps in your work history

▶ Dealing with sexual orientation bias

▶ Battling substance recovery shutout and handling assumptions about disabilities

. . . .

*T*he reasons candidates are rejected after interviewing (other than the commonly given reason of losing out to a better prepared or more qualified candidate) often relate to special situations. These range from a mild to a serious stumbling block in the interviewer's perception. Sometimes the special issues are discussed, but often they remain unspoken.

In this chapter, I cover how you can discuss and overcome these special issues.

Pulling Back the Curtain

Perhaps you've been in the same job too long, making you appear unmotivated. Maybe you have employment gaps or the opposite — too many previous jobs hanging around your neck.

Conceivably, you may be battling bias against a disability or sexual orientation. Could be that you're a woman who knows an underlying concern may be parental absenteeism — or whether you can supervise men. Or suppose you're crashing into brick walls because you're in alcohol- or substance-abuse recovery.

Sometimes you're pretty sure that you're running into rejection because you were fired or demoted. Or maybe you don't know what to say because you've been convicted of a crime.

Think carefully before discussing special issues. Even a question that seems innocent may cause you to reveal things you didn't mean to tell. For non-sensitive questions, asking for more time to think about your answer is okay. But for special-issue answers, you seem more straightforward and sure of yourself when you anticipate the question and are ready with a good answer.

Throughout this chapter, I provide comments and response strategies to help shape your special issue to your advantage.

When You've Long Been in the Same Job

What some may consider stability, others may see as fossilisation. Your chief strategy is to look industrious, ready to take on any challenge that comes your way, and be adaptable to new ideas. Here are some examples of *Show Stoppers* and *Clunkers and Bloopers* responses to a variety of questions you may be asked.

Because you've been with your last employer for so long, do you think you may have a hard time adjusting to a new company's way of working?

Show Stoppers

- ✔ Not at all. Give examples of how you've already learned to be adaptable — how your previous job was dynamic, provided a constantly changing environment and shared common links with the new company. Note parallels of budget, business philosophy and work ethics. You plan to take up mountain climbing and sky diving when you're 80 — figuratively speaking.

- ✔ Emphasise your commitment to your previous company as one of many assets you bring with you to the new position — and then name more of your assets.

Clunkers and Bloopers

> ✔ Discuss your relief at escaping that old, awful job — at last!
>
> ✔ Simply say you're ready to try something new.

You've been in your previous position an unusually long period of time — why haven't you been promoted?

Show Stoppers

> ✔ Present the old job in modules (by clusters of skills you developed instead of by your periods of employment). Concentrate on all increases in responsibility (to show upward mobility within the position) and on relevant accomplishments. Note raises.
>
> ✔ Say that you're interested in this new job precisely because of the inertia of your previous position. Mention any lifestyle changes (grown kids, second family income) freeing you to make a vigorous move at this time.
>
> ✔ Agree that your career hasn't progressed much, but note that many talented people are forced to accept lateral moves because few upwardly mobile job slots are available. Say your career plateau gave you time to reflect and solidify your skills set, lighting a fire under your motivation.
>
> ✔ Explain that you reached the highest position the company offered individuals in your specialty.

Clunkers and Bloopers

> ✔ Complain about office politics keeping you down.
>
> ✔ Say you were happy where you were and ask, 'Why fix what isn't broken?'

When You've Served Prison Time

For most jobs, you're not obliged to voluntarily disclose anything about your prior record, if you're not specifically asked to do so — although the specific circumstances of some positions may require disclosure. However, an employer can generally ask if you have a criminal record and may be entitled to refuse to employ you if you failed to answer a reasonable question, or gave a dishonest answer.

The key to dealing with prison time is to make the experience as positive as possible. Work double-time to outshine the other candidates with your positive outlook and qualifications for the job.

Here are several tips you may find useful:

✔ Generally, you're not required to disclose a *spent* conviction. Spent conviction schemes allow criminal record checks to be amended to remove references to some offences after a period of non-offending. However, some offences never become spent — for example, sex offences in some jurisdictions. Further, some kinds of employment, such as working with children, are exempt from spent conviction legislation. This means that employers are able to receive an employee's complete criminal record.

✔ In Australia, WISE Employment (www.wiseemployment. com.au) has 35 offices across the country and runs specialist ex-offender programs in Victoria and New South Wales. Their website also offers articles and resources.

✔ The Australian military does take into consideration the criminal history of applicants when assessing suitability; this is done on a case-by-case basis, and spent conviction legislation still applies. Similar standards apply for the New Zealand military, where all applicants undergo a police record check, and any convictions are assessed on the severity of the offence.

Tell me about your incarceration.

Show Stoppers

✔ Describe how it was one of the best learning experiences you've ever had. Explain the crossover (transferable) skills and education you acquired in prison.

✔ Say that it helped you make changes in your life so that the behaviour that got you in trouble is history. Part of your old problem was hanging out with the wrong people. In your new life, you hang out with a different group of people who don't get into trouble.

Clunkers and Bloopers

- ✔ Lie about your conviction, figuring no-one will learn about it until after you've been hired. (Why risk a firing on top of your criminal record?)

- ✔ Say you're a victim of bad police work and never should have been in prison (unless technology has cleared you of all charges).

When You're Shoved out the Door

The number-one rule in explaining why you were fired is to keep it brief, keep it honest and keep it moving. Say what you need to say and redirect the conversation to your qualifications. As for what you should say, you have two core options.

Were you fired from your last job?

Show Stoppers

- ✔ **If it wasn't your fault:** Explain the firing as a result of downsizing, mergers, company closure or some other act beyond your control. Sometimes firing happens several times in a row to good people who figuratively happen to be standing on the wrong street corner when the wrong bus comes along and runs them over. So many people have been on that bus these days that being terminated is no longer a big deal. Being let go wasn't your fault, so you have no reason to feel guilty. Get on with the interview with a sincere smile on your face.

- ✔ **If it was your fault:** Say you learned an enormous lesson during the experience. You messed up, but you know better now, and you won't make the same mistakes again. Explain briefly how you benefited from this learning experience. Then quickly turn the interview back to the better you and go on to explain how you're the hands-down best candidate for the job.

Sidelining a series of firings

If you've been fired from a significant number of jobs, few employers will be willing to give you a second chance. Understandably, they don't want to deal with the same problems your previous employers did.

Your best strategy is to call on a third party's help. Appeal to your family and friends to step in and recommend you to people they know personally who can hire you. Make sure that the people with hiring power are aware of your past mistakes, and assure them (honestly) that you've learned from the experiences and have reformed your wicked ways.

Your other most promising options are to obtain additional education or training for a fresh start. Or consider self-employment.

Clunkers and Bloopers

✔ Give interviewers the impression that you're hiding something, that you're not being absolutely honest and open with them.

✔ Bad-mouth your former boss. Say your former co-workers were a freak show.

✔ Tell the interviewer that you've had personality conflicts on more than one job. That admission sets off screaming smoke detectors warning that you're a fiery troublemaker.

Have you ever been asked to resign? Why?

Show Stoppers

✔ Being allowed to resign (a soft firing) suggests that you may be able to work out a mutually agreeable rationale with your former employer. Do so and stick to the story the two of you come up with.

✔ When you have no good storyline, admit your mistake and say it was a painful lesson that caused a change in your work habits.

Clunkers and Bloopers

> ✔ Lie or give excuses to justify why you shouldn't have been treated so unfairly.
>
> ✔ Moan about your ex-bosses or co-workers for forcing you out.
>
> ✔ Give multiple examples of your interpersonal conflicts.

When Sexual Orientation Is Up for Discussion

In Australia and New Zealand, getting a good job as an openly lesbian, gay, bisexual or transgendered (LGBT) candidate is much easier than in years past.

In an acknowledgment of changing times, for the first time ever, the United Nations in 2011 endorsed the rights of LGBT people in a resolution hailed as historic by Australia, New Zealand and other backers.

Here's expert Aussie career coach Kate Southam's take on the local situation. Many organisations understand the bottom-line benefits of having a diverse workforce, as well as the value of their employees bringing their authentic selves to work. For example, when LGBT non-profit organisation Pride in Diversity started in Australia in early 2010, the Australian Federal Police, KPMG, IBM, ING, Goldman Sachs and the Department of Defence were foundation members. And in New Zealand, legislation enabling same sex marriage was passed into law in April 2013, reflecting progressive social attitudes that extend to the workplace.

More answers to why you were fired

To see an additional 12 positive answers to the question 'Why were you fired?', visit my website, sunfeatures.com. Click Columns and, at the bottom of the left screen, click Good Answers to Hard Questions.

Observers of LGBT employment trends believe that the diversity message is now being received by not only big companies, but also many midsize companies too.

While a great deal of progress has been made to date, a group of interviewers — of all ages — continues to form the 'third rail' of interviewing for you. Because of their belief systems these interviewers operate with hard-wired predispositions against LGBT people, rain or shine.

Don't be lulled into complacency because of the rapid acceleration in the LGBT equality movement.

Be clear about your prospects

When you suspect that, for a screening interview, you've been paired with a closet homophobe whom you'll never see again, don't worry too much; that individual could be an anomaly. If the interviewer is the hiring manager to whom you'd report, worry.

As you evaluate how to move forward in your job search, note that a growing number of LGBT job seekers reject out of hand the notion of working for companies where they can't be open about their orientation. They say the effort to hide it takes a toll on their productivity, as well as their emotional and physical health.

But sometimes the need for employment takes over. When you can't find a workplace where your sexual orientation won't be used against you and you have rent or a mortgage to pay, you may choose not to disclose.

Disclosing is a highly personal choice

Here are suggestions to smooth away wrinkles from your interviewing experience:

- ✔ If you choose to disclose, wait until either the interviewer shows enormous interest in your qualifications and you know an offer is imminent, or the offer is actually made. Some savvy advisers recommend that you wait until you have a written offer letter in hand.

✔ Thoroughly research the company's culture and workplace policies before the interview. Look for companies that proclaim a non-discriminatory policy on sexual orientation.

✔ How can you tell whether equality happy talk is real or window dressing? Ask members of LGBT support networks what they know about a company where you plan to interview. Browse for LGBT job boards and websites.

✔ You may not choose to disclose at all. Many people just wait until a natural opener comes up at work after they are hired, such as talking about a partner or placing photos on a desk. Again, disclosing is a highly personal decision.

Although you won't be asked directly about your sexual orientation, an interviewer may — inadvertently or purposely — nibble around the edges with inappropriate personal questions.

Show Stoppers

Is there a special [member of the opposite sex] in your life? How's your marriage?

✔ *A nondisclosure answer:* You consider a number of women (or men) special in your life (meaning your mother or father, your sister or brother, and your aunt or uncle), or just say you're not married yet.

✔ *A confirming but neutral answer:* Say you're gay, open with your family and friends, and in a stable relationship. You may also want to casually mention that your sexual orientation has no bearing on the quality of your work. Add that it's not a problem for you and that you hope it isn't a problem for the company.

Being open suggests that you're not anxious and preoccupied about being exposed, that you have the support of your family, and that you're emotionally stable and strong.

Clunkers and Bloopers

✔ Bluntly refuse to discuss your personal life.

✔ Ask whether the interviewer is married.

In Australia and New Zealand, it would be pretty unusual for an interviewer to pose a question such as the preceding example to any candidate — whether heterosexual or LGBT. If such a question is asked, stay calm; the interviewer may be inexperienced or you may be learning something you need to know about the organisation — such as it's not for you.

I see that when you were a university student, you were president for two years of the campus gay advocacy group — can you tell me about that?

Show Stoppers

✔ Focus on the leadership and other skills you developed, such as fundraising, financial management and event planning. Explain briefly the work such groups perform across universities in Australia (or New Zealand). You could also outline the size of the membership you served and how as president you represented the organisation in student government, conferences and events, including hosting visiting dignitaries.

✔ Explain that, after leading the group as president for two years, you received a Campus Leader Award from the university's vice-chancellor; ask whether the interviewer would like to see it (from your portfolio).

Clunkers and Bloopers

✔ Answer only that it was a political action group for LGBT students.

✔ Say that you led protests at university events.

When You've Worked Everywhere

In an era of contract workers, just-in-time temporary hiring, and companies tossing employees overboard to boost profits for stockholders, I'm always surprised to hear employers object to 'job hopping'. I shouldn't be.

Employers favour candidates with a track record of staying a 'reasonable' amount of time at previous jobs. They assume that the past predicts the future and that the candidate will stay as long as she's wanted at the company.

The kicker is the meaning of 'reasonable amount of time'. The current group-think narrative places a minimum stay in a job at two to three years.

This arbitrary time frame doesn't mean that you shouldn't cut your losses and leave if you're in a bad job — circumstances vary widely. It does mean you need to give plenty of thought to how you handle a job-hopper question and deal with it in a logical, convincing and upbeat answer.

You've changed jobs more frequently than is usual — why is that?

Show Stoppers

> ✔ List accomplishments in each job that relate to the position you seek. Note that you built new skills in each job. Say that you're a person who contributes value wherever you go.

> ✔ Give acceptable, verifiable reasons you changed jobs so frequently — project-oriented work, downsizing, dead-end positions, company sold out or department shutdown.

> ✔ Say that you've become more selective lately, and you hadn't been able to find the right job until this opportunity came along; explain your employment travels as a quest for a fulfilling job.

> ✔ If this move is a career change for you, show how your experience and skills support this change and how the position fits your revised career goals.

> ✔ If your positions were for temporary agencies, cluster the jobs by responsibility and recast them as evidence of your use of cross-functional skills in many situations.

> ✔ Ask whether this is regular-status employment. If so, admit you've lacked some commitment in the past, but now you're ready to settle down with a good company, such as this one. If not, say a temporary job is just what you have in mind to keep your skills refreshed with experiences gained at various companies.

Clunkers and Bloopers

> ✔ Complain about what was wrong with each of your ex-employers that made you quit. Say you didn't want to waste your time working for dysfunctional people and organisations.

> ✔ Show a lack of focus — you just couldn't get into your jobs.
>
> ✔ Say you're looking for something that pays more.

When Gaps Drill Holes in Your History

Employers may rush to judgement when they find gaps in your job history.

If your job history has as many gaps as a footy player's smile, try to find growth experiences (self-directed study or education by travel).

If you must blame your jobless patches on sick leave, emphasise that you have fully recovered and are in excellent health. If personal problems take the hit (ill parent or sick child), follow up with facts that indicate the personal problems are history.

When your record is spotty beyond belief, try to get on with a temporary job and then prove by your work record that you've turned over a new leaf.

Sometimes the gaps in your record are of recent vintage — you've been looking for employment without success for a very long time. In current periods of unemployment, your posture is commitment — you throw yourself heart and soul into your work and you want to be very sure to find a good fit. Explain your waiting period as a quest for a fulfilling job.

How long have you been job hunting? Wow! That's a long time — what's the problem? Why haven't you had any job offers yet?

Show Stoppers

> ✔ Say you've become more selective lately, and you hadn't been able to find the right job until this opportunity came along.
>
> ✔ If you were given a sizeable severance package, explain how it financially allowed you to take your time searching for the perfect next move.

✔ Admit your career hasn't progressed as much as you'd like, but you've had time to think through your life direction, you've reassessed your career and you feel focused now. You're fuelled up and ready to go!

✔ Explain that while you're good at building consensus (through compromise) with others, you haven't been willing to settle for a job that doesn't maximise your skills and qualifications. Clarify that you've taken your time to find the perfect job fit because the position is very important to you.

Clunkers and Bloopers

✔ Say you don't know what the problem is — employers or recruitment companies never respond to your job applications.

✔ Complain about the low quality of the roles available in the current job market. (You could just sound bitter.)

✔ Gripe about how many opportunities you've missed out on because recruiters don't recognise your true worth.

✔ Look depressed and admit that you're becoming discouraged.

When You're Demoted a Notch

Demotion carries more negative baggage than does firing. Demotion suggests personal failure; firing doesn't, unless you're fired for cause.

Do I read this resume right — were you demoted?

Show Stoppers

✔ Your best move is to deal with demotions before you reach the interview. Ask your demoting boss for a positive reference and come to an agreement about what happened that's favourable to you — assuming your boss knows you're looking around and doesn't mind helping you leave.

✔ Explain honestly and as positively as possible the reasons for your send-down.

✔ Admit that you weren't ready for the responsibility at that time, but now you are. Describe the actions you've taken to grow professionally — courses in deficient areas, management seminars and books, and introspection.

✔ Affirm that you're looking for a good place to put your new and improved management skills to use, and you hope that place is where you're interviewing. Quickly remind interviewers that you're qualified for the job you're interviewing for, and back that up with examples of your skills and quantified achievements.

Clunkers and Bloopers

✔ Lie or try to shift the blame to ABY (anybody but you).

✔ Accuse management of unreasonable expectations.

When People in Recovery Interview

Networking is the way many people in substance recovery get job interviews, with the result that the referring party often has revealed your background to the interviewer.

When you're sure that the interviewer is well aware of your substance history, find a way to introduce the topic on your terms: *I am a better-than-average qualified candidate for this job. As you know, I have fought the substance abuse battle and won.*

Emphasise that you are a battle-tested, proven individual who has survived, taken control of your life and grown into a stronger person. Try not to become mired in interminable details of your recovery, but stick to your main theme of being a well-qualified applicant who overcame an illness and is now better equipped to meet new challenges than most people.

As soon as you think you've tapped in to the interviewer's sense of fairness, redirect the conversation to reasons you should be hired. But until you calm the interviewer's anxiety about your recovery, the interviewer won't truly hear anything you say about your strengths and qualifications.

Seek more advice on doing well in job interviews when you have red flags such as drug or alcohol abuse in your background. Read *Job Interview Tips for People with Not-So-Hot Backgrounds* by Ron and Caryl Krannich, PhDs (Impact Publications).

Head-on questions in a job interview are unlikely to be asked — *Do you drink more than you should? Do you use drugs?* But you may be indirectly questioned.

We have a drug testing policy for all employees. Do you object to that?

Show Stoppers

- ✔ Answer that, no, you certainly don't object. You could add details such as that you don't use drugs or alcohol. You're in a recovery program and have been substance-free for a year (or more). Discuss your qualifications for the position.

- ✔ Add that you have no health problems that would prevent you from giving 100-per cent effort on every assignment.

Clunkers and Bloopers

- ✔ Say you're doing your best to get your life back together; to prove it, you've attended four rehab programs in the past two years. You just need a chance at a good job to keep you clean (sober).

- ✔ Say you had some problems in the past, and give no details about how you kicked substance abuse.

When Women Are Put on the Spot

News flash! Young women of child-bearing age often have to deflect questions about family matters.

Research companies for family-friendly policies before you apply. For example, the Workplace Gender Equality Agency website in Australia (www.wgea.gov.au) or the Female Friendly websites in Australia and New Zealand (www.femalefriendly.com.au and femalefriendly.co.nz) list companies considered employers of choice for gender equity. Recommendations from people in your network and articles published by women's media, including websites and magazines identifying the best companies that promote work–life balance, are also valuable. Use your networks and search for stories in local newspapers and on their websites to find similar small and midsize companies where you live.

When you have small fry and you choose to stay home with them, but you still need the pay, contemplate alternatives: working part-time, pairing up with another person to do the same job (job sharing), taking your work home (telecommuting), and rearranging work schedules without cutting productive hours (flexitime).

In the meantime, standard responses to the subtle (or not-so-subtle) probes about the patter of little feet: Kids are way, way in the future because (say why); you value your career and want to continue to progress; the lifestyle you'd like to grow accustomed to requires a two-income family; you have super-reliable child care (explain).

When cornered, try this tactic to ensure you won't become a staffing problem down the line: *Whether or not I plan to have children in the future is not central to my career. Like so many other energetic women today, I intend to work and have a career no matter what happens in my personal life.*

What are your career plans?

Show Stoppers

- ✔ This job meets your immediate career plan. It allows you to be a solid producer yet build on your already strong skills. You will work hard at this job to prove yourself and accept greater responsibility as it is offered. You're reasonably ambitious. You don't plan to relocate.

- ✔ Making career plans five years out is not realistic in today's rapidly changing job market. But you're excited about developing new green technology [or whatever], and this job is exactly what you seek. Your background makes you a perfect fit (provide details).

Clunkers and Bloopers

- ✔ You expect a promotion within a year (suggesting that you'll be unhappy if you don't quickly rise through the ranks).

- ✔ You don't have a particular goal in mind.

What is your management style?

Show Stoppers

> ✔ Explain how your management style is compatible with the company culture (you researched that culture on the company website). Incorporate contemporary management-style language (you read a few magazines and recent books on the language of business today). No marbles in your mouth when you state how you handle insubordination, motivation, serious mistakes and other supervisory issues.

> ✔ Explain that you don't flinch at making tough decisions and implementing them. But you're not a bully or micromanager. You empower and motivate staff to promote productivity. Storytell: Give true examples of how you've handled past supervisory problems.

Clunkers and Bloopers

> ✔ Give a vague answer on management style, revealing your naiveté.

> ✔ Out-macho a male interviewer or seem to be too lightweight for the job.

When Disabilities Are Revealed

Australian and New Zealand anti-discrimination laws severely limit what interviewers can ask people with disabilities prior to offering a job.

Essentially, an interviewer can ask you about your abilities to perform a job, but not about your disabilities. Questions on your state of health may be asked in some circumstances. For example, interviewers can ask about your fitness level if you're going for a job requiring physical ability such as child care or warehousing where you may be required to lift and carry. Interviewers are also allowed to invite prospective employees to disclose to them any illness, injuries or disability that may inhibit their capacity to perform the job.

An employer discriminating on the grounds of disability is generally not unlawful if

- ✔ The employee can't perform the *inherent requirements* of the job as a result of the disability.

- ✔ Providing services or facilities required by the employee in order to carry out the inherent requirements of the job imposes an *unjustifiable hardship* on the employer.

So if you have a visible disability, you may benefit by giving an explanation of how you're able to do the job.

For a quick brush-up on your rights in job interviews, check out the Australian Human Rights Commission (www.humanrights. gov.au) or the New Zealand Human Rights Commission (www.hrc.co.nz).

Examples of questions to expect include the following:

You say you can do the job. How would that work? Can you explain more?

Show Stoppers

- ✔ When practical, ask to give a demonstration — if need be, bring your own equipment.

- ✔ When a demonstration is impractical, pull an example from your last job (paid or volunteer) or educational experience. Storytell: Recount a true tale of your having been there, done that.

- ✔ Anticipate essentials to job performance (anything in the job description) the interviewer may be worried about — such as physical mobility, safety and motor coordination. If you have a vision or hearing impairment, expect some concerns that you'll miss visual or aural cues essential to job performance. Explain how you've adapted in these areas or will overcome obstacles.

- ✔ Suggest a few references (previous teachers, counsellors, employers, or co-workers) who can testify to your abilities to do the job.

Clunkers and Bloopers

- ✔ Show you're offended by the question — soapbox about unspoken bias.

- ✔ Explain that your co-workers have always set aside their work to assist you with problematic tasks.

- ✔ Without examples to support your claims, assert you have no problems with job performance.

Because you're our first applicant with a disability, we've never dealt with accommodations before. What are these accommodations likely to be?

Show Stoppers

- ✔ Do your homework and outline requirements, particularly where they are minimal. Give examples of how your skills will merit the company's small investment.

- ✔ Offer to provide some of your own equipment (you aren't required to do so, but the offer shows serious interest in contributing to the company).

- ✔ Offer information on accommodations, such as contact details for government agencies and companies that provide devices or consulting services. Government agencies include Disability Services Australia and the Ministry of Social Development in New Zealand's Mainstream Employment Programme.

Clunkers and Bloopers

- ✔ Name a costly price for all the equipment you could possibly need, assuming the company can afford the expense.

- ✔ Act demanding because you think that the anti-discrimination laws are protecting you — the interviewer on the lookout for litigious types won't hire a bad attitude.

- ✔ Cite the requirements of the anti-discrimination act relevant in your area and threaten to sic your lawyer on them. If you sue, hope you win enough money to not need a job — ever!

Chapter 19

Answering a Questionable Question

Is that a Korean name?

What year did you graduate from high school?

Are you a Christian?

*A*ll these questions are foolish ones in a job interview. Every human resources specialist in Australia and New Zealand knows this. But unsophisticated interviewers who don't deal with employment issues on a regular basis often cross the line and ask personal, intrusive and discriminatory questions.

Employers shouldn't quiz you about any of the following topics:

✔ Age

✔ Birthplace

✔ Colour

✔ Disability

✔ Marital/family status

✔ National origin

✔ Race

✔ Religion

✔ Sex (gender)

✔ Sexual orientation

Laws in Australia and New Zealand prohibit employers from asking certain questions unrelated to the job they're hiring to fill. Questions should be job related and shouldn't be used to pry loose personal information. Some inquiries about the off-limits topics are flat-out illegal. Others are merely borderline and inappropriate. This chapter helps you recognise both types of employment probes and suggests responses to make honey out of none-of-your-beeswax questions.

Defining Illegal Questions

An *illegal* question is one that the interviewer has no legal right to ask.

The New Zealand government and Australian federal government have laws restraining employers from asking intrusive questions. These laws cover age, sex, religion, race, ethnicity, sexual orientation, and so forth. Asking illegal questions can get the interviewer called on the legal carpet.

To find out what's what, get ahead of the game and research the facts:

✔ In Australia, check out the Australian Human Rights Commission website (www.humanrights.gov.au) for useful articles as well as details of anti-discrimination laws that apply in your state or territory.

✔ In New Zealand, head straight to the New Zealand Human Rights Commission website (www.hrc.co.nz) and click on the Enquiries and Complaints tab, where you can find a list of FAQs on the left side of the page. Click on Job Application Questions to access a general guide to what can and can't be asked, and to download a more detailed booklet — just look for the 'Getting a job: An A–Z for employers and employees' link.

✔ Browse online for 'list of illegal job interview questions'.

Defining Inappropriate Questions

An *inappropriate* question is one the interviewer can technically ask but probably shouldn't. Depending on whether the information is used to discriminate, inappropriate questions set up employers for lawsuits. Inappropriate questions range from anti-discrimination and privacy issues to hard-to-classify bizarre inquiries:

> *Is your partner female?*
>
> *How would you go about making a pizza?*
>
> *If you were at a departmental meeting and a co-worker put his hand on your thigh, what would you do?*

Interviewers in companies that have human resources departments should know better than to ask inappropriate questions. But some go on fishing expeditions, hoping that weird, unexpected questions will rattle candidates, causing them to 'show their true colours'.

Other interviewers are natural-born troublemakers who ask risky questions because they want the information and are willing to gamble that they won't be challenged.

Illegal questions are always inappropriate, but inappropriate questions are not always illegal.

Think First, Answer Second

What if an interviewer does cross the line and has the audacity to toss you a possibly discriminatory question? Assuming that you want the job, think through your answer before automatically flaming the transgressor with snarky responses like the following:

> *Is your question aimed at trying to find out how old I am? That would be illegal. Shame on you!*
>
> *As you know, under federal law, basing employment decisions on gender is illegal, and I feel that this question is discriminatory in nature.*

Those up-front comebacks work only in the movies. It's a mistake to verbally punch out an interviewer — especially if the interview is otherwise going well and you're sensing that this job could be the right one for you. The interviewer may not be typical of the sort of people you will work for or with.

Having said that, if a question is repugnant or blatantly discriminatory, don't answer it at all — or answer it your way. For example, an answer to the question mentioned earlier in this chapter — *Is your partner female?* — may be this one:

> *I don't feel that specific details of my personal life would be appropriate to discuss here. They do not affect my ability to effectively perform the duties of this position. (Translation: Back off.)*

Sometimes you have to establish your boundaries firmly. But in general, if you want the job, avoid becoming confrontational and answer all the questions to your benefit.

But what if the interviewer would be your boss and is such a jerk that you don't want the job? Utter a polite exit line and leave.

Redirect Inappropriate Questions

As well as responding to an inappropriate question by establishing your boundaries (refer to preceding section) another, foxier approach can work better for you, especially if you think the interviewer's questions come from ignorance rather than bias. Deftly twist the offensive question. Here's an example of redirecting:

Suppose the interviewer asks a question about age:

> *I see you went to the University of Queensland. My son's there now. When did you graduate?*

The smooth candidate directly responds to the question, sort of:

> *I don't think your son and I know each other. I'm sure he's a fine young man. As for me, fortunately, I've been out of university long enough to have developed good judgement. Would you like to know a little about how my good judgement saved a previous employer $25,000?*

Another way to redirect is to answer the question you want to answer, not necessarily the question that's asked. (Politicians do so all the time.) Using the same situation, here's an example of how a smooth candidate cherry-picks the conversation:

> *You mention the University of Queensland, such a fine school. In addition to taking my undergraduate degree there, I have since returned there to complete an intensive executive management course that prepared me for exactly the kind of position we're discussing now. Would you like to hear more about how I'm a good match for the financial oversight functions of this position?*

You know that religion is a slippery-slope question not to answer directly. But the question may come at you sideways. Suppose, for example, you're asked whether you'll need time off to celebrate any religious holiday. Try this approach:

> *I understand your concern about the time I will need to observe my religious beliefs, but let me assure you that if this time has any bearing on my job performance at all, it will only be positive, because the inspiration of my beliefs will help me stay renewed, fresh and mentally focused.*

My suggested answer makes no mention of specific religious holidays, it doesn't refuse to answer, and it doesn't confront the interviewer with the discriminatory nature of the question.

(Obviously, if you're interviewing at a religious organisation known for restricting hiring to its faith's followers and you're one of their faithful, identify yourself.) As a rule, you win by remaining calm and out-thinking an offensive questioner. A good job offer is the best interview strategy of all.

Rehearsing Dicey Questions

Table 19-1 is a playbill of inappropriate or illegal questions you hope you never hear. Decide in advance how you'll respond to nonstarters like these — just in case. When the quizzing is expressed in an appropriate version, give a straightforward answer.

Table 19-1 Questions Interviewers Shouldn't Ask

Topic	Inappropriate or Illegal Questions	Appropriate Versions
Age	What is your date of birth?	If hired, can you furnish proof that you are over age 18?
	How old are you?	None.
Arrest and conviction	Have you ever been arrested?	Have you ever been convicted of a crime? If so, when, where, and what was the disposition of the case?
Citizenship/national origin	What is your national origin? Where are your parents from?	Are you legally eligible for employment in Australia (or New Zealand)?
Disabilities	Do you have any disabilities?	Can you perform the duties of the job you are applying for?
Education	When did you graduate from high school or university?	Did you complete your final year of high school? Do you have a university or college degree?
Family	How many children do you have?	What hours and days can you work?
	Who's going to babysit? Do you have preschool-age children at home? What is your marital status? Do you have caring responsibilities? Are you looking after your aged parents?	Do you have responsibilities other than work that will interfere with specific job requirements, such as travelling?

Topic	Inappropriate or Illegal Questions	Appropriate Versions
Home	Do you own your home?	None.
Language	What is your native language? How did you learn to read, write or speak a foreign language?	Which languages do you speak and write fluently? (If the job requires additional languages.)
Military record	What type of discharge did you receive?	What type of education, training and work experience did you receive while in the military?
Organisations	Which clubs, societies and lodges do you belong to? Are you a union member?	Are you a member of an organisation that you consider relevant to your ability to perform the job?
Personal	What colour are your eyes and hair? What is your weight?	Permissible only if there is a bona fide occupational qualification.
Pregnancy	Your application says that your status is married. Do your plans include starting a family soon?	None.
Religion	What is your religious denomination or religious affiliation? What church do you attend? What is your parish? Which religious holidays do you observe?	Are there specific times you cannot work?
Worker's compensation	Have you ever filed for worker's compensation? Have you had any prior work injuries?	None. None.

Part V
The Part of Tens

the
part of
tens

Enjoy an additional (and free!) online Part of Tens
chapter. Visit www.dummies.com/extras/
successfuljobinterviewsau.

In this part...

- ✔ Show off your star quality and win rave reviews for your interview performance with sure-fire tips and techniques.

- ✔ Find your way through tricky questions and interview challenges that may go against the standard script.

Chapter 20

Ten Ways to Win Rave Reviews

· ·

· ·

*J*ust like with movies that are on the nose, rotten reviews affect job interviewees too, even though shortcomings in the performances don't become public in a newspaper or on a website. When interviewees just don't hear back, they feel the same way as panned actors: Awful.

Don't let that unhappy ending happen to you. Do everything you can to make your interview performance earn rich reviews. And to help, in this chapter I share ten ways you can do just that from a master of job search, career coach Joe Turner (www. jobsearchguy.com).

Master the Art of Storytelling

An interview is a conversation. Don't fall into an answers-only rut. Spend time learning to storytell with true prepared stories that highlight your accomplishments.

Need more encouragement? Studies suggest that people remember stories better than other forms of communication. As Mark Twain, himself no slouch as a storyteller, said, 'Don't say the old lady screamed — bring her on [stage] and let her scream.'

In short, an interview is a conversation. An employment conversation is a series of questions and answers. As soon as you answer a question, try following up with a question of your own.

Go in Knowing Your Lines

About 90 per cent of candidates 'didn't get the wiki' that their purpose in an interview is to do infinitely more than ask for a job. Not you. You got the wiki.

Your goal is two-fold: First, you want to demonstrate that you are a good 'fit' for the organisation — like salt and pepper, bread and butter, *The Chaser* and satire.

Second, you're looking for breaking news on whether the position is really something you want to invest a chunk of your life in.

Leave the Begging to Others

Neediness is one of the all-time deal killers in the job market. Whisper in your own ear before walking in the door: 'I don't need this job. I do need air, food and water.' Keep things in perspective. Sell your strengths and your ability to do the job.

Employers don't hire because they feel sorry for you; they hire because they want you to solve *their* problems.

Share the Stage with Dignity

Generally, you want to participate in an interview as an equal, not as a subordinate of the person conducting the interview. Of course, you should still show courteous respect to the interviewer, especially if the interviewer is a general and you're a buck private.

Participating as an equal is a subtle matter of self-perception, so remind yourself of your status before the interview begins.

Perform with Confidence

From the moment you walk into an interview room, demonstrate confidence. Your first impression makes a difference. Stand up straight, make eye contact and offer an enthusiastic handshake with your interviewer. If you don't remember names well, jot down the interviewer's name on your notepad as soon as you're seated. Ditto for any other person you're meeting with.

Avoid Ad Libbing Ad Infinitum

Although you should always do your share to keep the conversational flow going, droning on loses your audience. Telling your interviewer more than she needs to know can be fatal.

Your stories should be no longer than 60 to 90 seconds, and they must — repeat, *must* — have a relevant point related to your topic. Stick with your rehearsed stories, your research, your adequate answers and the questions you need to ask.

You're looking for an easy give-and-take in your interview without coming across as a motormouth.

Keep in Mind the Interviewer Is Not Your New Best Friend

Don't make the mistake of being overly familiar. A good interviewer is skilled enough to put you at ease within the first ten minutes of the interview. That doesn't mean the interviewer has become your best friend. Never let your guard down.

Remember that you're there to give and receive information about a position that you may want. From start to finish, treat this encounter as the professional business meeting that it is.

Know That Faulty Assumptions Equal Faulty Interviewing

Think about this scene on a stage: The leading female actor is supposed to rush to the leading man as he enters stage right; for some reason, he enters stage left and she rushes to an empty space. She looks as though she doesn't know what she's doing.

The same is true when you make a wrong assumption about what your interviewer has in mind with a particular question. When in doubt, ask! You don't lose points in an interview for asking questions when you don't clearly understand a point.

Keep Emotions out of the Interview

Sure, this may be a time of stress in your life. The rent's due, the car's on the fritz or you recently had an argument with your significant other.

Put it all behind you while you're on stage in the spotlight. Here's why: The interviewer may at times consciously attempt to provoke you into a temperamental outburst. Don't fall for it or take it personally. It may be only a part of an overambitious interviewing process.

Remember, your role is to be cool, calm and collected — so play the part. When emotions enter an interview, failure follows.

The Power of Asking Questions

You want to be sure you're getting the true picture of what this job is really about and whether you want it. Arrive with a list of several prepared questions about the company, the position and the people who work there.

Ask questions that begin with 'what', 'how' and 'why'. Avoid questions that require a simple 'yes' or 'no' response. Take notes.

Most interviewers are unimpressed by a candidate who has no questions. They wonder whether you're uninterested, have no sense of curiosity, are not too bright — or think you already know everything.

Chapter 21

Ten (Or So) Tricky Questions to Watch Out For

*T*ricky questions look like one thing and turn out to be something very different.

A tricky question can cause you to admit something the interviewer believes to be true but isn't. As a single example, the interviewer may use the verbal construction of a 'loaded question', such as the classic 'Do you still beat your wife?' In this illustration, the questioner assumes that you have beaten your wife in the past.

However phrased, a tricky question may seem like slam-dunk material but, in reality, it's a double-faced probe that presents great risk to your chances of being hired. Think before talking. *Be sure you know what's really being asked.*

What's the best job interview response to all questions? It's the one that adds up to 'Hire me!' As Sherlock Holmes would say, 'Elementary, Dr. Watson.' But recruiters report that high numbers of job seekers blab negative information without realising they're making a farewell address to a job opportunity.

In this chapter I cover ten prime-time tricky probes with hidden agendas that experienced interviewers use to separate the possible hires from the rejects.

Why've You Been Out of Work so Long?

Another question along these lines could be 'How many others were laid off?' or 'Why you?'

Why is the interviewer asking you about your recent employment history when you've already said you were laid off (not fired)? This quizzing could cause you to reveal something that's wrong with you that other employers have already discovered.

The interviewer is fishing to determine whether there was a layoff of one and you were it. Or whether your former manager used the theme of recession and budget cuts to dump groups of second-string employees.

The 'Hire me!' answer: Explain that, after your layoff, you stopped to re-evaluate where your life is headed. You began your search in earnest only a few weeks ago, when you realised your true aims. The interviewer's company and this position are of special interest to you.

An alternative explanation for not jumping into the job chase centres on a time-out event that has since resolved itself — an ill family member, for instance.

Any direct answer to why you were included in a reduction in force is risky because anger toward your former managers could pop up, raising doubt about your self-control. A better idea: Punt. Shake your head and say you don't know the reason, because you were an excellent employee who gave more than a day's work for a day's pay.

If Employed, How do You Manage Time for Interviews?

The real question is whether you're lying to and short-changing your current employer while looking for other work.

Clearly state that you're taking personal time, and that's why you interview only for job openings for which you're a terrific match.

If further interviews are suggested, mention that your search is confidential and ask if it would be possible to meet again on a Saturday morning or after normal working hours. You are not a time cheater. You are not a slacker. You are not a liar.

How Did You Prepare for This Interview?

Translation: Is this job important enough for you to research it, or are you going through the motions without preparation, making it up as you go?

You very much want this job, and of course you researched it, starting with the company website. For other pointers, look back at Chapters 5 and 15.

Do You Know Anyone Who Works for Us?

If a company has a nepotism policy prohibiting the hiring of relatives, you'd be aware of it and not wasting everyone's time by interviewing.

But the friend question is a two-way street. Nothing beats having a friend deliver your resume to a hiring manager, but that transaction presumes the friend is well thought of in the company. If not — ouch!

Remember the birds-of-a-feather rule: Highlight a friend inside the company only if you're certain of your friend's positive standing.

Where Would You Really Like to Work? Doing What?

The real agenda for this question is assurance that you aren't applying to every job opening in sight, that you actually know what you want, and that you won't be bored stiff by the job being discussed.

Caveat: Never, ever mention another company's name or another job.

A short 'Hire me!' answer is a version of the following: 'This is the place where I want to work, and this job is what I want to do. I have what you need, and you have what I want. I can't wait to get to work here.'

What Bugs You about Co-workers or Bosses?

This not-so-subtle inquiry is a clever trap to see if you're a troublemaker or have a prickly personality.

Steer clear of this third-rail territory. Develop a poor memory for past irritations. Reflect for a few moments, shake your head, and say you can't come up with anything that irritates you. Continue for a couple of sentences elaborating on how you seem to get along with virtually everyone.

Mention that you've been lucky to have good bosses who are knowledgeable and fair, with a sense of humour and high standards. Past co-workers are able, supportive and friendly. Smile your most sincere smile. Don't be lured into elaborating further.

Can You Describe How You Solved a Work/School Problem?

This forthright question is tricky only in the sense that most job seekers can't come up with an example on the spot that favourably reflects on their ability to think critically and develop solutions.

The answer is obvious: Anticipate a question about how your mind works and have a canned answer ready. A new graduate might speak of time management to budget more time for study; an experienced worker might speak of time management to clear an opportunity for special task force assignments.

Can You Describe A Work/School Instance In Which You Messed Up?

The question within a question is whether you learn from your mistakes or keep repeating the same errors. A kindred concern is whether you're too self-important to consider any action of yours to be a mistake.

Speaking of mistakes, here's a chance to avoid making one during your job interview: Never deliver a litany of your personal bad points. Instead, briefly mention a single small, well-intentioned goof and follow up with an important lesson learned from the experience.

How Does This Position Compare With Others You're Applying For?

A similar question could be 'Are you under consideration by other employers now?'

The intent of these questions is to gather intel on the competitive job market or get a handle on what it will take to bring you on board. Maybe the job market for your talents is flat and you can be had on the cheap. Or if your resume is parked at several companies, why haven't you been snatched up?

You can choose a generic strategy and say you don't interview and tell, and that you respect the privacy of any organisation where you interview, including this one. Emphasise that this company is where you hope to find a future and ask, 'Have I found my destination here?'

If You Won The Lottery, Would You Still Work?

This question goes to your motivation, work ethic and enthusiasm for work. Are you merely occupying a space until you can hang it up?

A possible answer: If you mean it, say yes, you'd retire right now. But since you need to work, this is the sort of work you prefer.

The 'Hire me!' answer: While you'd be thrilled to win the lottery, you'd still seek out fulfilling work because working, meeting challenges and scoring accomplishments are what make most people happy, including you. Say it with a straight face.

When You're Uncertain

If a hardball question comes at you out of left field, try not to panic. Take a deep breath, look the interviewer in the eyes and comment that it's a good question you'd like to mull over and come back to. The interviewer may forget to ask again.

But if the question does resurface and your brain goes on holiday, say that you don't know the answer and that, being a careful worker, you prefer not to guess.

If you've otherwise done a good job of answering questions and confidently explained why you're a great match for the position, the interviewer probably won't consider your lack of specifics on a single topic to be a deal breaker.

Index

Notes

Notes

....

Notes

About the Author

Joyce Lain Kennedy is America's first nationally syndicated careers columnist. Her twice-weekly column, 'Careers Now', appears in newspapers and on websites across the land. In her four decades of advising readers — newbies, prime-timers and those in between — Joyce has received millions of letters inquiring about career moves and job searches, and has answered countless numbers of them in print.

Joyce is the author of seven career books, including *Joyce Lain Kennedy's Career Book* (McGraw-Hill), *Electronic Job Search Revolution*, *Electronic Resume Revolution*, and *Hook Up, Get Hired! The Internet Job Search Revolution* (the last three published by John Wiley & Sons).

Writing from Carlsbad, California, a San Diego suburb, Joyce is a graduate of Washington University in St. Louis.

Author's Acknowledgements

The richness of helpful information you find within these pages is due to my luck in sourcing many respected minds in the employment space. Contributors to whom I am especially indebted are individually credited in chapter pages. Applause to one and all.

Additionally, thanks a billion to the following individuals who worked long and hard to make this book happen:

James M. Lemke, above-the-title technical advising star and executive world traveler, who is indispensable to the quality of every book I write.

Lindsay Sandman Lefevere, For Dummies executive editor, who is godmother for this book and quite a few others.

Linda Brandon, top editor at the top of her game, who attentively shepherded this book through a myriad of publishing hoops, always making valuable suggestions.

Melanie Astaire Witt, writer and editor, who provided inordinate expertise to produce this book's first appendix of interview questions by career fields and industries.

Yevgeniy 'Yev' Churinov, computer whiz and social networking guru, who contributed both technological clarity and practical production assistance to this work.

Krista Hansing, copyeditor of the first rank, who used her sharp eyes, sound judgment, and commitment to the project to make this a far better book.

Gail Ross, literary agent-attorney and longtime friend, who continues to help me make the right publishing moves.

Publisher's Acknowledgements

We're proud of this book; please send us your comments through our online registration form located at dummies.custhelp.com.

Some of the people who helped bring this book to market include the following:

Acquisitions, Editorial and Media Development

Project Editor: Charlotte Duff

Acquisitions Editor: Clare Dowdell

Editorial Manager: Dani Karvess

Production

Graphics: diacriTech

Technical Reviewer: Kate Southam, James M. Lemke

Proofreader: Kerry Laundon

Indexer: Don Jordan, Antipodes Indexing

The author and publisher would like to thank the following copyright holders, organisations and individuals for their permission to reproduce copyright material in this book:

• **Cover image:** © Jamie Grill Photography/Getty Images

Every effort has been made to trace the ownership of copyright material. Information that enables the publisher to rectify any error or omission in subsequent editions is welcome. In such cases, please contact the Legal Services section of John Wiley & Sons Australia, Ltd.

Business & Investing

978-1-74216-998-9
$45.00

978-1-118-22280-5
$39.95

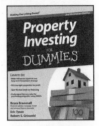
978-1-118-39670-4
$39.95

978-0-73030-584-2
$24.95

978-1-74216-971-2
$39.95

978-1-74246-896-9
$39.95

978-1-11857-255-9
$34.95

978-0-73037-807-5
$29.95

Reference

978-1-118-49327-4
$34.95

978-1-118-30525-6
$19.95

978-0-730-30780-8
$24.95

978-0-7303-0442-5
$24.95

Order today! Contact your Wiley sales representative.

e Available in print and e-book formats.

A Wiley Brand

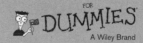

Fitness

Aussie Rules For Dummies,
2nd Edition
978-0-7314-0595-4

Cycling For Dummies,
Australian & New Zealand Edition
978-0-7303-7664-4

Fishing For Dummies,
2nd Australian &
New Zealand Edition
978-1-74216-984-2

Fitness For Dummies,
Australian & New Zealand Edition
978-1-74031-009-3

Pilates For Dummies,
Australian Edition
978-1-74031-074-1

Rugby Union For Dummies,
2nd Australian &
New Zealand Edition
978-0-7303-7656-9

Weight Training For Dummies,
2nd Australian &
New Zealand Edition
978-1-74031-044-4

Yoga For Dummies, Australian &
New Zealand Edition
978-1-74031-059-8

History

Australian History For Dummies
978-1-74216-999-6

Australian Politics For Dummies
978-1-74216-982-8

Indigenous Australia For Dummies
978-1-742-16963-7

Kokoda For Dummies,
Australian Edition
978-0-7303-7699-6

Tracing Your Family History Online
For Dummies,
Australian Edition
978-1-74031-071-0

Health & Health Care

Beating Sugar Addiction
For Dummies, Australian &
New Zealand Edition
978-1-118-64118-7

Being a Great Dad For Dummies
978-1-742-16972-9

Breast Cancer For Dummies,
Australian Edition
978-1-74031-143-4

Dad's Guide to Pregnancy
For Dummies, Australian
& New Zealand Edition
978-0-7303-7735-1

Food & Nutrition For Dummies,
Australian & New Zealand Edition
978-0-7314-0596-1

IVF & Beyond For Dummies,
Australian Edition
978-1-74216-946-0

Kids' Food Allergies For Dummies,
Australian & New Zealand Edition
978-1-74246-844-0

Living Gluten-Free For Dummies,
Australian Edition, 2nd Edition
978-0-730-30484-5

Menopause For Dummies,
Australian Edition
978-1-740-31140-3

Pregnancy For Dummies,
3rd Australian & New Zealand
Edition
978-0-7303-7739-9

Type 2 Diabetes For Dummies,
Australian Edition
978-1-118-30362-7

Reference

Cryptic Crosswords For Dummies
978-1-118-30521-8

English Grammar For Dummies,
2nd Australian Edition
978-1-118-49327-4

English Grammar Essentials
For Dummies, Australian Edition
978-1-118-49331-1

Freelancing for Australians
For Dummies
978-0-7314-0762-0

Passing Exams For Dummies,
2nd Edition
978-0-730-30442-5

Solving Cryptic Crosswords
For Dummies
978-1-118-30525-6

Successful Job Interviews
For Dummies, Australian &
New Zealand Edition
978-0-730-30805-8

Writing Essays For Dummies
978-0-470-74290-7

Writing Resumes & Cover Letters
For Dummies, 2nd Australian &
New Zealand Edition
978-0-730-30780-8

Order today! Contact your Wiley sales representative.

 Available in print and e-book formats.

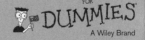

For Dummies is a registered trademark of Wiley Publishing Australia Pty Ltd